MW01257451

# NEVERMORE!

## Edgar Allan Poe • The Final Mystery

by

JULIAN WILES

**Dramatic Publishing**
Woodstock, Illinois • London, England • Melbourne, Australia

This play is dedicated to its original cast and crew,
who suffered through revision after revision and took each
one as a challenge. The final version, published here,
is a tribute to their dedication, creativity and friendship.

The opening performance of *NEVERMORE!* took place on October 14, 1994 at the Charleston Stage Company, Charleston, South Carolina, with the following cast:

*Agatha Blackwell* ..................... Lady in Mourning
*William Brown* ............Homer Walker, Roderick Usher,
Viscount Valequez, Priest
*John Carroll* .................Captain Jeremiah Reynolds
*Marianne Clare* ......................... Young Annabel
*Donald Curry*...............................Dr. Nicolai
*Allston DuPre* .....................Cabin Boy, Acolyte
*Nancy Fiedler* ..Aunt, Mrs. Reilly, Duchess Ulrica, Barmaid,
Mourner
*Margaret Ford* ................ Lady in Crimson, Mourner
*Janice Friedman* ..... Lady in Green, Madame L'Espanaye,
Mourner
*Dominique Gillard* ...........Cabin Boy, Hopfrog, Acolyte
*Sid Katz* ... Aaron Abrams, Inspector Grimke, Prince Prospero,
Bartender, Mourner
*Christopher Kolb* ...................... Rusty, Pallbearer
*Brooke Haynie* ................. Jake, Legrand, Pallbearer
*Aaron Heisler* ...............................Pallbearer
*Josiah Longshanks*........................Gravedigger
*Jennifer Metts* ...........................Annabel Lee
*Byron J. Miller* ..Master of Ceremonies, Constable Ross, Query
*Barbara Nicolai* ..... Mrs. Prothero, Mrs. O'Leary, Mourner
*Dustan Nigro* .........................Edgar A. Perry
*Hadley Owen* ............Lady in Purple, Hannah O'Leary,
Mademoiselle Camille L'Espanaye, Mourner
*Frank Parsons* ........................... Dr. Fleming
*Rowand Robinson* ................... Miguel, Pallbearer
*Don K. Savelle* ........................Captain Nimrod
*Ian Walker* ...........................Edgar Allan Poe
*Sarah Wyckham* .............................Mourner

# NEVERMORE!

## A Full Length Play
### For 12 Men and 7 Women, playing 52 roles

## CHARACTERS

<u>Five lead characters are disguised as other characters:*</u>
YOUNG POE *(Edgar A. Perry)
YOUNG ANNABEL LEE *(Disguised Mourner)
ANNABEL LEE *(Disguised Lady in Mourning)
EDGAR ALLAN POE *(Disguised Gravedigger)
CAPT'N. NIMROD *(Disguised Dr. Nicholai)
CAPT'N. JEREMIAH REYNOLDS *(Disguised Dr. Fleming)


<u>Also, several characters double roles:</u>
HOMER WALKER / RODERICK USHER / VISCOUNT
        VALEQUEZ / PRIEST / CABIN BOY / ACOLYTE
AUNT / MRS. REILLY / DUCHESS ULRICA / BARMAID /
        MOURNER
LADY IN CRIMSON / MOURNER / LADY PROSPERO /
        MRS. QUERY
LADY IN GREEN / MME L'ESPANAYE / MOURNER
CABIN BOY / HOPFROG / ACOLYTE
AARON ABRAMS / INSPECTOR GRIMKE / PRINCE
        PROSPERO / BARTENDER / MOURNER
RUSTY / PALLBEARER
JAKE / LEGRAND / PALLBEARER
FATHER / PALLBEARER
MASTER OF CERMONIES / CONSTABLE ROSS /
        MR. QUERY
MRS. PROTHERO / MRS. O'LEARY / MOURNER
LADY IN PURPLE / HANNAH / MLLE L'ESPANAYE /
        MOURNER
MIGUEL / PALLBEARER

# ACT ONE

### SCENE 1: The First Mystery Was His Name

*On the Beach at Sullivans Island, South Carolina*

*(A mysterious mist enshrouds the stage. A VISION IN WHITE materializes from the darkness and crosses D.)*

ANNABEL LEE.
>Mystery...
>In the end there was only mystery.
>We know he boarded a ship bound for New York
>But where he journeyed on that final fateful voyage no
>>one knows...
>...the true destination, a mystery.
>That was Eddie,
>He lived a life of mystery.
>I think that's what drew me to him
>The mystery...the imagination...
>You have to make your own truth he once told me...
>And he did...

*(Once ANNABEL crosses D, the U curtain falls U of it and dancers gather.)*

When I first met him, he had even fabricated a new name for himself...Edgar A. Perry, he called himself...Sergeant Major Edgar A. Perry...He had run away from home, changed his name and joined the army...He was stationed at Ft. Moultrie, on Sullivans Island. He was already over-

7

whelmed by his imagination...He said he was twenty-two but he was actually, only eighteen. Oh, the imaginary worlds he conjured up! Said he'd taken a mysterious trip to Russia and Greece which was, of course, all fancy...One could scarcely believe anything he said. But that night...at the Regimental Ball, when he asked me to dance...I believed every word he uttered...(*A dance ensues. The silhouettes of couples waltzing about the floor are projected on the U curtain.*)

## SCENE 2: I'll Love You Forever

*Ballroom at the Lee House on Sullivans Island*

*(YOUNG EDGAR A. PERRY, Poe at about seventeen, appears in front of the U curtain. He sweeps YOUNG ANNABEL LEE, also seventeen, off her feet and whirls around the dance floor... after a few turns he pulls her off to one side.)*

EDGAR A. PERRY. I'll love you forever...

YOUNG ANNABEL LEE. Mr. Perry, we've only just met...

EDGAR A. PERRY. Destiny has brought us together...we will never part...

YOUNG ANNABEL LEE *(teasing him)*. Never part?

EDGAR A. PERRY. Not till the end of time...Not even then.

YOUNG ANNABEL LEE. Who are you?

EDGAR A. PERRY *(grandly, outrageously)*. I am Sergeant Major Edgar A. Perry, Defender of Sullivans Island.

YOUNG ANNABEL LEE. Are you always this incorrigible?

EDGAR A. PERRY. Always. Besides, we poets are always incorrigible.

YOUNG ANNABEL LEE. Oh, you're a poet as well...

EDGAR A. PERRY *(nods "yes")*. All men are poets at heart.

YOUNG ANNABEL LEE. I'd like to read one of your poems...

EDGAR A. PERRY. And you shall, as soon as I write one...

YOUNG ANNABEL LEE. Tell me, Mr. Perry, do you ever speak the truth?

EDGAR A. PERRY. Only in desperation...Why rely on ordinary truth when we can create our own reality?

YOUNG ANNABEL LEE. An interesting point of view...

EDGAR A. PERRY. Oh, it serves you well, you should try it...

YOUNG ANNABEL LEE. For instance?

EDGAR A. PERRY. For instance, if you are spoken for... *(YOUNG ANNABEL LEE goes to answer but PERRY puts his finger to her lips.)* pretend you are not...that you are still free.

YOUNG ANNABEL LEE. Well—

*(Her FATHER enters.)*

FATHER. She *is* spoken for, sir...

EDGAR A. PERRY *(challenging the intruder)*. And who are you...

FATHER. I am her father...Come, my dear...*(Her FATHER parts them, gives PERRY a look, then leads YOUNG ANNABEL away.)*

EDGAR A. PERRY. But I don't know your name...

FATHER *(turns back to PERRY with a glare)*. And you don't need to. Come along, Annabel. *(They start off.)*

YOUNG ANNABEL LEE *(calling after him).* Annabel...Annabel Lee. *(PERRY takes a step toward them but FATHER turns, stops and blocks him.)*

EDGAR A. PERRY. What a lovely name!

FATHER. Sir, kindly retire, my daughter has nothing more to say to you.

EDGAR A. PERRY. Sir, I would like to ask for her hand...

FATHER. Are you mad, boy?

EDGAR A. PERRY. There are those that think so, sir...

FATHER. Come along, Annabel...*(YOUNG ANNABEL, led by her FATHER, exits.)*

*(The VISION IN WHITE reappears.)*

ANNABEL. Eddie appeared on our doorstep everyday but Father forbade me from admitting him...and I always obeyed my father...of course, Father said nothing about chance meetings on the beach...*(As ANNABEL crosses D the sound of the ocean is heard.)*

### SCENE 3: "I Was a Child, She Was a Child"

*On the Beach at Sullivans Island*

*(Moonlit night. Projections of leaves appear on the U curtain. Behind it Annabel's bedroom is being set up. EDGAR A. PERRY appears from the shadows.)*

EDGAR A. PERRY. Annabel...

YOUNG ANNABEL LEE. I shouldn't have come...

EDGAR A. PERRY *(teasingly).* But...

YOUNG ANNABEL LEE. You're wicked, Sergeant Perry...
do you know that?

EDGAR A. PERRY. What can I say? I'm a poet...

YOUNG ANNABEL LEE. So you claim, sir...

EDGAR A. PERRY. Well, I will make good my claim with...
*(He writes in the sand. As he writes, YOUNG ANNABEL
reads.)*

YOUNG ANNABEL LEE. I was a child and she was a child,
You think I'm a child?...

EDGAR A. PERRY. Children of Eros we are...

    I was a child and she was a child,

    In this kingdom by the sea: *(He writes in the sand again.)*

YOUNG ANNABEL LEE *(reads again)*. But we loved with a
love that was more than love—

EDGAR A. PERRY *(reading as he writes)*. I and my—

YOUNG ANNABEL LEE *(reading as he finishes writing the
line)*. Annabel Lee...*(Touched, turning to him.)* Eddie...

EDGAR A. PERRY. Close your eyes...

YOUNG ANNABEL LEE. Why?

EDGAR A. PERRY. I have a present for you...now close
them...

YOUNG ANNABEL LEE. All right...

EDGAR A. PERRY. Now, hold out your hand...

YOUNG ANNABEL LEE. Pray, what kind of present have
you for me...gold, diamonds...

EDGAR A. PERRY *(holds his hand high over hers and pours
a thin stream of sand from his hand to hers)*. Eternity.

YOUNG ANNABEL LEE *(opens her eyes and looks at the
sand and then deeply into his eyes. He smiles)*. Eternity...

FATHER *(from offstage)*. Annabel...Annabel...

YOUNG ANNABEL LEE. Father, I gave him the slip...I
must go...

EDGAR A. PERRY. Give him the slip again...

YOUNG ANNABEL LEE. I can't...

FATHER *(offstage)*. Annabel...*(YOUNG ANNABEL gives PERRY a kiss and then exits into the darkness. As lights fade on PERRY, YOUNG ANNABEL reappears in a spot on the other side of the stage.)*

ANNABEL. I disappeared into the shadows, shadows from which I would never return. That summer, a dark cloud swept over our mystical kingdom by the sea...a cloud— malarial fever...fever, fever so fierce that the city was in a panic. Guards were posted at the doorways of houses, houses which were afire with the pestilence. One of the houses was mine. No one was allowed to come in and out...but this didn't stop Eddie. He climbed a live oak near the back piazza and made his way to my room. Father was not pleased.

*(U curtain rises to reveal Annabel's bedroom.)*


**SCENE 4: Is There Any Hope?**

*Annabel Lee's Death Bed*

*(YOUNG ANNABEL lies near death in a bed UL. Her FA-THER and a matronly AUNT are DL conferring. Through the window U, PERRY appears. He tiptoes to YOUNG ANNABEL's side.)*

EDGAR A PERRY. Annabel...

FATHER *(discovering him)*. Sir, you have no place here.

EDGAR A PERRY. I love her, sir, I will not be dissuaded...

FATHER. I must ask you to withdraw. She's very near death. She is delirious. She doesn't know any of us anymore...

EDGAR A PERRY. Dear God, is there no hope?

FATHER. None...

YOUNG ANNABEL LEE. Eddie...Eddie, is that you?

EDGAR A PERRY *(crosses and kneels by her side).* Annabel...

YOUNG ANNABEL LEE. I knew you would come...

EDGAR A PERRY. You must hold on...You're going to get well. We're going to be together...

YOUNG ANNABEL LEE. Oh, Eddie, if that only that could be true.

EDGAR A. PERRY. We must make out own truth, remember?

ANNABEL. I remember...

EDGAR A. PERRY. Promise me you'll never leave me.

YOUNG ANNABEL LEE. Not till the end of time.

EDGAR A. PERRY. Not even then...

YOUNG ANNABEL LEE. Not even then...I have something for you, take this...*(She thrusts a handful of paper into his hands.)* It's my turn to give you a present...

EDGAR A. PERRY. They're blank...*(She nods "yes." Smiles.)* What must I do with them?

ANNABEL. Fill them with wonder...*(She drifts off again.)*

FATHER. Perhaps we should let her rest now...*(PERRY nods. FATHER and AUNT exit. PERRY lags behind to give YOUNG ANNABEL a final kiss. He then crosses D. As he does, the U curtain falls behind him and as he crosses farther D, the D curtain falls behind him. As he recites, the Poetry Lecture is set up behind the D curtain and the ship's gang plank is set up behind the U curtain.)*

EDGAR A. PERRY.
>Take this kiss upon the brow!
>And, in parting from you now,
>Thus much let me avow

>. . . . . . . . . . . .
>Yet if hope has flown away
>In a night, or in a day,
>In a vision, or in none,
>Is it therefore the less *gone*?
>*(He continues DR and speaks to the audience.)*

## SCENE 5: The Poetry Lecture

EDGAR A. PERRY.
>I was a child and *she* was a child,
>>In this kingdom by the sea:
>But we loved with a love that was more than love—
>>I and my ANNABEL LEE;
>With a love that the winged seraphs of heaven
>>Coveted her and me.

>And this was the reason that, long ago,
>>In this kingdom by the sea,
>A wind blew out of a cloud, chilling
>>My beautiful ANNABEL LEE;
>So that her high-born kinsman came
>>And bore her away from me,
>To shut her in a sepulcher
>>In this kingdom by the sea.

*(Lights crossfade from PERRY to EDGAR ALLAN POE, DL, now 40. He picks up the lines at this point.)*

EDGAR ALLAN POE.

For the moon never beams, without bringing me dreams
Of the beautiful ANNABEL LEE;
And the stars never rise, but I feel the bright eyes
Of the beautiful ANNABEL LEE;
And so, all the night-tide, I lie down by the side
Of my darling—my darling—my life and my bride,
In the sepulcher there by the sea,
In her tomb by the sounding sea...

*(The D curtain rises behind him to reveal that the scene has been transformed to a poetry lecture.)*

So you see, the most precious things in this life are the things we have lost...Poetry is a quest to recover those lost moments, for the poet gives us a brief and indeterminate glimpse of what lies beyond our reach, beyond the grasp, beyond our comprehension

...a glimpse of immortality...glimpses, all too brief...

When we find ourselves melted into tears from a poem it is not because of its beautiful words, it is from the sorrow we feel...sorrow at our inability to grasp here on earth, the rapturous joys of the divine...so we hunger, we thirst for another glimpse. And like the moth dancing about a candle flame, if we are not careful, we will be consumed by our desire.

MASTER OF CEREMONIES. Thank you, Mr. Poe...This concludes Mr. Poe's lecture, and although he has a steamer for New York to catch tonight, he has agreed to accept a few questions...

LADY IN GREEN. Mr. Poe, this new poem seems to contradict *The Raven*, in that the bereaved lover in *The Raven* is told he will never see his true love again, here in *Annabel Lee*, you profess that true love lives on, beyond the grave...

POE. Yes...

LADY IN GREEN. But isn't that a contradiction?

POE. Yes...

LADY IN GREEN. Well, would you like to clear up the contradiction?

POE. No...*(He takes a flask from his pocket and drinks. The audience of LADIES is shocked.)*

LADY IN CRIMSON. Mr. Poe, don't you believe in temperance...

POE. Of course, my dear, after all I'm a member of the Sons of Temperance...and I drink to them every chance I get... *(He drinks again, LADIES gasp.)*

MASTER OF CEREMONIES. Yes, well, I think we best get Mr. Poe off to his waiting boat...*(POE is pulled from the stage.)*

LADY IN GREEN. Shocking...

LADY IN CRIMSON. A troubled genius...

LADY IN PURPLE. I heard last year he attempted suicide... over a woman...

LADY IN GREEN. Which one?...I hear he's proposed to five women just in the past few weeks...*(POE and the MASTER OF CEREMONIES pass by and as they do, POE drinks again.)*

LADY IN PURPLE. Cad...

LADY IN GREEN *(as she and the LADIES cross D)*. Drunkard...

LADY IN CRIMSON. Blue-eyed mad is what I hear...*(LADIES exit. POE and the MASTER OF CEREMONIES cross*

*D and the D curtain falls behind them. While the scene continues, the poetry lecture set is struck.)*

MASTER OF CEREMONIES. Yes, well, we do appreciate your taking the time to lecture to us, Mr. Poe, and as promised, here is a token of our appreciation. *(He gives POE an envelope of bills.)* I must tell you, however, that we would have appreciated your lecture more if you had not been in such an inebriated condition...

POE. Well, I charge double for sober lectures...

MASTER OF CEREMONIES. Indeed...

POE. Did you enjoy my lecture, Reynolds? Mr. Ives, have you met my friend, Captain Jeremiah Reynolds? He's down from New York...

MASTER OF CEREMONIES. Jeremiah Reynolds, the Antarctic explorer?

REYNOLDS. The same...

MASTER OF CEREMONIES. An honor, sir. Perhaps you could lecture for us sometime...

POE. Do you think you could make the same kind of impression as I made tonight, Reynolds?

REYNOLDS. It would not be easy, to outdo you, Edgar.

POE. Can I buy you two gentleman a drink? I noticed a tavern across the street.

REYNOLDS. Edgar, we have a boat to catch.

POE. Oh, yes, Captain Reynolds here is taking me to New York tonight. He promised me that if I journey to that great metropolis on the Hudson that he would tell me of his most recent South Polar adventures.

MASTER OF CEREMONIES. I am honored to meet you both but I don't want you to miss your boat, so I'll say good night.

REYNOLDS. Good night, sir.

POE. Here's to you. *(Drinks from his pocket flask.)* What time does our ship sail?

REYNOLDS. Midnight. *(Ship's whistle sounds. D and U curtains rises on the next scene.)*


### SCENE 6: "We've Been Expecting You"

*On Baltimore Dock*

*(The gangplank of the ship. A few SAILORS are about and at the top of the gangplank, two CABIN BOYS mill about, waiting on the final passenger. Above, the Raven cries. DL, POE and REYNOLDS enter. The CABIN BOYS recognize POE and cross D to meet them.)*

CABIN BOY 1. Mr. Poe?

POE. Yes?

CABIN BOY 2. We've been expecting you, sir. *(He takes POE's bag then pokes the other CABIN BOY who runs up the gangplank to alert the CAPTAIN that POE has arrived.)*

POE. Is it midnight already?

CABIN BOY 2. Nearly that, sir.

POE. Time and tide wait for no man, I suppose.

*(CAPTAIN NIMROD comes down the gangplank.)*

CAPTAIN NIMROD. Jeremiah...

REYNOLDS. Amos...

CAPTAIN NIMROD. And this must be the illustrious Edgar Allan Poe.

REYNOLDS. Edgar, this is an old friend of mine, Captain Amos Nimrod.

CAPTAIN NIMROD. This is indeed a pleasure, Mr. Poe. I'm one of your most devoted readers.

POE. Are you?

CAPTAIN NIMROD. Indeed I am. It will be a pleasure to have you aboard.

POE. I'm sure the pleasure is all mine, sir.

CAPTAIN NIMROD. Well, do come aboard.

POE. Thank you.

CAPTAIN NIMROD. Oh, Jeremiah, I've arranged for you and Mr. Poe to dine with me tonight. I've invited a few select passenger to dine with us...

POE. Dine? Now? Tonight?

CAPTAIN NIMROD. I know it's late, but seeing your name on the manifest, everyone wanted to wait dinner on you...

POE. Well, our bags...

CAPTAIN NIMROD. The boys will see to your bags and I'll take you directly to dinner...

POE. Actually, I...

CAPTAIN NIMROD. I think, Mr. Poe, you will be especially pleased with the wine selection. *(They go up the gangplank onto the ship. As they do, two SAILORS in long capes who have been standing guard at the bottom of the gangplank turn and we see they are skeletal creatures. They walk up the gangplank and prepare to pull it up. As they do, lights fade. The Raven cries out in the darkness. The U curtain falls and projections of ship's rigging appears on it.)*

**SCENE 7: "We Have Two Distinguished Guests"**

*The Captain's Table*

*(GUESTS gather about in the Captain's cabin. They are having drinks before dinner. CAPTAIN NIMROD, at a table, is tapping into a cask of wine one of the CABIN BOYS has brought in.)*

CAPTAIN NIMROD. Ladies and gentlemen, we have two distinguished guests aboard tonight, the Antarctic explorer, Captain Jeremiah Reynolds...*(DINNER GUESTS applaud.)* and an explorer of the dark recesses of the human mind, Mr. Edgar Allan Poe. *(Pouring a glass for POE.)* And in celebration of these illustrious personages, I have broken into the fine shipment of wine aboard. Mr. Poe, I think you will find our selection especially interesting...

POE *(drinks)*. Amontillado? It can't be...*(Pronounced a-mon-ti-ya-do.)*

CAPTAIN NIMROD *(to one of the LADIES)*. We have five casks of amontillado aboard...

POE. How on earth did you manage it?

CAPTAIN NIMROD. Oh, we sea captains have our ways...

REYNOLDS *(sipping his wine)*. Delicious...

OTHERS *(ad lib)*. Yes, yes, delicious...

MR. AARON ABRAMS. Before you arrived, Mr. Poe, we were discussing your stories. It seems we all have a favorite...Mine is *The Telltale Heart*, The captain fancies *The Pit and the Pendulum* and Mrs. Reilly there, is quite enamored with *Masque of the Red Death*...

MRS. REILLY *(approaching POE)*. Oh, yes...

CABIN BOY 2. I like *Hopfrog*...you know the one with the dwarf...*(Others laugh.)*

MRS. REILLY. It appears that everyone is reading your stories.

POE. My publishers certainly hope so.

MRS. REILLY. Mr. Poe, are you working on a new story at present?...

POE. The stories work on me, my dear. They stalk me, demanding to be written...and when I can stand it no longer, I commit them to paper...

MRS. PROTHERO. Wherever do you find the inspiration for them?

REYNOLDS. Yes, set our minds at ease, Edgar, for there are those who believe that you consort with the devil. *(The CAPTAIN laughs gently.)*

POE. There are those that think I am the devil himself.

CABIN BOY 1. Are you? *(All laugh.)*

POE. You flatter me, son...No, I am not that gentleman...

CABIN BOY 2 *(to CABIN BOY 1)*. Good.

MRS. REILLY. But are there demons that possess you when you write, Mr. Poe?

POE. We all have our demons, Madame...

MRS. PROTHERO. So you believe in spirits...

POE. Oh, yes, I do believe in spirits...*(Indicating the wine by holding up his goblet.)* What shall we drink to...life?

CAPTAIN NIMROD *(joining the group. Quickly, mischievously).* Why not death?...I believe that is one of your main preoccupations, Mr. Poe...

POE *(uneasily, doesn't quite know what to make of NIMROD).* Yes, well, death is one of my preoccupations, I suppose...among others. *(He raises his glass, others follow. They toast and drink.)*

MRS. PROTHERO. You're so mysterious, Mr. Poe.

POE. I've always been drawn to the obscure and the mysterious, Madame. Mystery drew me to Captain Reynolds. His expeditions to the mysterious South Polar regions served as an inspiration for my character of Arthur Gordon Pym, a man who dares to explore the unexplored.

MRS. REILLY. ...Oh, I can hardly believe this, the author and his inspiration right here at the same table...

REYNOLDS. I fear we are found out, Edgar...

POE. Alas...*(POE and REYNOLDS toast.)*

REYNOLDS. Edgar did exaggerate my voyages a bit.

POE. Artistic license...

MRS. PROTHERO. Why do you take such risks, Captain Reynolds, to explore such a desolate and unknown place as the Antarctic?

POE. It is the unknown places, the *terra incognita*, that draw us, Madame...

REYNOLDS. Yes, Madame, we want to unravel the mysteries of our world.

MRS. PROTHERO. Indeed! Well, then, perhaps, Captain Reynolds, you could unravel one for us. Could you tell us why you wore just one glove to dinner tonight?

REYNOLDS. Alas, Madame, like many adventurers in the Antarctic, I am a victim of frostbite. My hand, I fear, might prove too distressing for certain parties.

MRS. PROTHERO. Heavens...

REYNOLDS. A small price to pay for discovery...

MRS. REILLY. Earlier, Mr. Poe, Captain Reynolds told us he believes that somewhere in the South Polar region, past the ice floes, there lies the entrance to another world.

POE. Have you discovered the entrance to another world, Jeremiah?

REYNOLDS. Yes.

POE. What does it lead to? Heaven...or hell?

REYNOLDS. That remains to be seen. On my last expedition, we got within seven hundred miles of the South Pole itself,

and the sailors whom I had hired in Patagonia said they
had once been even closer and the tales they told...

POE. Tales?

MR. HOMER WALKER. Do you discount them, Mr. Poe?

POE. Oh, I am not one to throw suspicion on the tales of
others. *(All laugh.)*

MRS. PROTHERO. Would you recite something for us, Mr.
Poe?

MRS. REILLY. Oh yes, please...

POE. Really, if you will forgive me...

MRS. REILLY. Please.

MRS. PROTHERO. You must.

REYNOLDS. I fear, Edgar, you will seem inhospitable if you
refuse the ladies.

MRS. PROTHERO. Oh no...please do not disappoint us...

POE. Thank you, but it is late...

MRS. REILLY. Please...how often do we have a writer in
our midst?

REYNOLDS. They shall never let you go, Edgar...

MRS. PROTHERO. Just a poem...

POE. Just a poem? You do not know, my dear, how danger-
ous just a poem can be...

MRS. PROTHERO. Dangerous?

POE. Doorways to disaster.

MRS. REILLY *(aside)*. Whatever is he talking about?

POE. Poetry and literature are the windows and doorways that
open into the nether realms. We poets seek to open the
windows of light but too often, we, like Pandora, break
open the doorways of darkness, unleashing into our world
shadowy creatures of evil...creatures like the Raven...*(The
Raven cries but only POE can hear him. There is a mo-
ment of uncomfortable silence, the crowd murmurs, and
then POE, very slowly, very softly, begins to recite.)*

Once…upon a midnight dreary, while I pondered…
   weak…and weary,

Over many a quaint and curious volume of forgotten
   lore—

While I nodded, nearly napping, suddenly there came a
   tapping,

As of some one gently rapping, rapping at my chamber
   door.

" 'T is some visitor," I muttered, "tapping at my chamber
   door—

     Only this and nothing more."


Open here I flung the shutter, when, with many a flirt
   and flutter,

In there stepped a stately Raven of the saintly days of
   yore.

. . . . . . . . . . . . . . . . . . . . . . . . . . . . .

Perched upon a bust of Pallas, just above my chamber
   door

     Perched, and sat, and nothing more…


. . . . . . . . . . . . . . . . . . . . . . . . . . .

"Tell me what thy Lordly name is on the Night's
   Plutonian shore!"

     Quoth the Raven, "Nevermore."


"Prophet!" said I, "thing of evil!—prophet still, if bird
   or devil!

By that Heaven that bends above us—by that God we
   both adore—

Tell this soul with sorrow laden if, within the distant
   Aidenn,

It shall clasp a sainted maiden whom the angels name
Lenore."
    Quoth the Raven "Nevermore."

"Be that word our sign of parting, bird or fiend!" I
shrieked, upstarting—
"Get thee back into the tempest and the Night's
Plutonian shore!
Leave no black plume as a token of that lie thy soul
hath spoken!
Leave my loneliness unbroken!—quit the bust above
my door!
Take thy beak from out my heart, and take thy form
from off my door!"
    Quoth the Raven "Nevermore."

*(Everyone applauds but all POE hears is the cry of the
Raven, high above.)*

I cracked the door of darkness and gave wing to this evil
thing...now he pursues me...pursues me...*(Screaming
madly to the Raven that the others cannot see.)*

    Fiend...I created thee!

    Get thee back into the tempest and the Night's Plutonian
shore!

LADIES *(in background, ad lib).* Is he still quoting from the
poem?...He scares me...Me, too...

CAPTAIN NIMROD. Perhaps, ladies and gentlemen, it being
late we should adjourn...

ALL *(ad lib).* Yes, yes...Good night, Mr. Poe...*(All except
REYNOLDS withdraw.)*

REYNOLDS. Edgar...are you all right...?

POE *(taking a drink).* No...he pursues me, day and night.

REYNOLDS. The raven?

POE *(desperately, grabbing hold of REYNOLDS).* Yes. He's
sunken his claws into me and won't let go...not since, not
since that night. I hadn't written in months and I feared I'd
never write again...One night after an evening of libations,
I made my way back to my rooms...I grabbed up paper
and pen determined to write again...but nothing would
come...nothing...I took up a new sheet of paper, then an-
other...There is nothing more terrifying than an empty
piece of paper, Jeremiah, lying there taunting you, daring
you, cursing you...laughing, for it knows that all the while
it remains barren, it is tormenting you. And that night, that
night, the torment was especially intense, hellish...Fool-
ishly, I said I would do anything to write again...any-
thing...and then, the words came, a watershed of wonder.
Every drop of ink that fell from my pen, I tell you, was
brilliant, brilliant...but I shuddered at the sight. It was my
life's blood itself that was dripping on the page. A poem of
despair...of love, eternal love obliterated...and I knew, the
moment it was finished, that it was the devil's work. *(He
drinks.)*

REYNOLDS. Edgar, you sell yourself short.

POE. Yes, I did sell myself short...*(He goes from glass to
glass, drinking the remains of the drinks others left be-
hind.)* a great reputation...a brilliant career...and a dark
shadow over my soul...so I don't write anymore for fear
that what I write will be the devil's work...and because I
don't write...*(The Raven cries in the distance, POE drinks
again.)* he pursues me. He comes to settle up...to claim my
soul. *(He takes a drink.)*

REYNOLDS. Get a hold of yourself, man...

POE *(desperately grabs REYNOLDS's hand).* I know my time
is near, Jeremiah. I can feel the Angel of Death breathing
down my neck. *(He drinks again.)*

REYNOLDS. I think perhaps you just need a good night's sleep.

POE *(grabbing REYNOLDS's arm tighter)*. No, I am pursued by demons in my sleep...so I don't sleep...My only rest is in a stupor that consumes more of me than I of it...Once I could keep the demons at bay with pen and paper...No longer, no longer...I fear the terrors I might write.

REYNOLDS. Come now, you'll write again...

*(NIMROD enters, unseen by POE.)*

POE *(desperate)*. No, I will never again do the devil's work... *(Drinks again.)* besides...my hand shakes so...I could only make scribbles on the page...*(He takes a drink, then another, then another, and finally passes out.)*

CAPTAIN NIMROD. It seems our guest is a bit under the weather.

REYNOLDS. Yes, a little under the weather.

*(CABIN BOYS 1 and 2 enter.)*

CAPTAIN NIMROD. Take him to his cabin.

CABIN BOYS. Yes sir. *(As lights fade, they take POE off to his cabin. The Raven cries.)*

### SCENE 8: The Telltale Heart

*Poe's Cabin Aboard the Ship*

*(The projections of ship's rigging are replaced with projections of portholes. A bed is brought on to C and a table*

*and chair placed L. CABIN BOYS 1 and 2 enter and put POE in bed, then exit through the door. Lightning and thunder appear outside the portholes and POE awakens, looks about the unfamiliar surroundings. Lightning and thunder crash again. POE staggers to sit up in bed.)*

POE *(running his hand through his hair)*. A midnight dreary...*(Lightning and thunder crash once more, he finds his pocket flask, takes a drink, then falls back into his bed. There is a knock at the door. POE stirs.)* Go away. *(Another knock.)* Oh, please...*(He staggers to his feet.)* Who's this rapping at my chamber door? Is it the wind and nothing more—

*(INSPECTOR GRIMKE and CONSTABLE ROSS, followed by MRS. O'LEARY and her daughter, HANNAH, enter from the DC trapdoor, as if they are coming from downstairs.)*

CONSTABLE ROSS. Sorry to bother you so late at night, sir, but I'm afraid there has been a complaint. *(Crosses past POE to C.)*

POE. A complaint?

INSPECTOR GRIMKE. Yes sir. If you please, sir, a word with you...*(Crosses to ROSS at C.)*

POE. A word with me...*(Looks to GRIMKE and ROSS.)*

CONSTABLE ROSS. Is there no one else here?

POE *(crosses to GRIMKE at C)*. Not that I know of...why? *(ROSS looks around, crosses to Poe's bed.)*

INSPECTOR GRIMKE. We have reason to believe there was some kind of altercation here tonight.

POE. An altercation?

CONSTABLE ROSS *(who's been snooping about Poe's belongings, faces POE)*. You say there's no one else about, now?

POE *(crosses R of GRIMKE to ROSS)*. No...*(ROSS is looking under Poe's bed. POE turns to GRIMKE.)*...now if you would kindly explain...

INSPECTOR GRIMKE *(crosses to table and looks at papers there)*. Tell me, sir, how long have you been in your room, tonight?

POE. In my cabin? Well, actually, gentlemen, I don't exactly know. *(GRIMKE and ROSS exchange glances.)*

CONSTABLE ROSS *(takes step toward POE)*. Do you have *some* idea?

POE *(crosses to ROSS)*. Well, I didn't reach the ship until midnight...I dined with the other passengers...I fear I may have had too much to drink *(Faces GRIMKE.)* and when I awoke I was here.

INSPECTOR GRIMKE *(looking up from his investigation of the contents of Poe's desktop)*. What ship, sir?

POE. What ship? Why, *this* ship.

ROSS *(makes a note)*. Subject thinks he's on a ship.

POE *(to ROSS)*. Of course I'm on a ship...*(Crosses to GRIMKE.)* What's going on? Who are you?

INSPECTOR GRIMKE *(crosses around desk toward POE)*. Inspector Grimke and that's Constable Ross there.

POE. Well, if you would please explain.

CONSTABLE ROSS *(crosses D but stays a step U of them)*. Mrs. O'Leary, is this your boarder?

MRS. O'LEARY. Yes, that's the scoundrel. He and the other gentleman came in around midnight.

POE *(a step toward her)*. Who are you, Madame?

MRS. O'LEARY *(crosses to POE at C)*. Don't you pretend not to know me, sir. You let these rooms from me three weeks ago. *(Crosses to GRIMKE.)* I was suspicious all along. I never would have let to him but Hannah felt sorry for him, said he looked like a wet puppy there on the doorstep.

POE *(faces GRIMKE)*. I have never seen these ladies before in my life.

MRS. O'LEARY *(to GRIMKE)*. He's been drinking, hasn't he? *(Crosses to face ROSS.)* I run a respectable boarding house, I do. *(Crosses to POE.)* I told you I wouldn't tolerate no liquor under my roof. Demon rum always leads to trouble in boarders. *(Crosses to ROSS.)* Kindly get him out of my house, Constable...*(ROSS starts for POE.)*

INSPECTOR GRIMKE *(crosses to C)*. A moment...please. First, we need you to tell us the whereabouts of the other gentleman.

POE *(crosses to GRIMKE)*. I don't know anything about another gentleman.

CONSTABLE ROSS. Did you and he have a quarrel?

POE *(faces ROSS)*. A quarrel? No...*(A step toward ROSS.)* ...look...

INSPECTOR GRIMKE *(a step toward POE)*. These ladies heard noises.

MRS. O'LEARY *(leaning over toward ROSS.)* Disturbing noises. *(Turns back to give HANNAH a nod.)*

CONSTABLE ROSS. Coming from your room.

POE *(crosses R of GRIMKE)*. I don't know anything about—

INSPECTOR GRIMKE *(crosses to MRS. O'LEARY)*. Ladies, perhaps you should describe what you heard.

MRS. O'LEARY. It was Hannah that heard it. *(She pushes HANNAH in front of her.)* Go on, now, Hannah. Tell 'em what ya heard.

HANNAH. If you please, sir, it was a fight, a tussle. I could hear the sound of something or someone being thrown about and raised voices and then a thud and then silence...

INSPECTOR GRIMKE. Is that when you called your mother?

HANNAH. Well, I was too scared to move at first and then after I didn't hear anything else for a while I thought maybe I'd been...

MRS. O'LEARY. Dreaming.

HANNAH. Dreaming!

POE *(folds arms, looks out front)*. Perhaps she was.

HANNAH. I thought so, too. *(Long pause.)* But then I heard another sound.

INSPECTOR GRIMKE. Another sound?

HANNAH. Yes, like someone chopping firewood...You know that sound when you chop up fat litard?*

CONSTABLE ROSS. Fat litard?

HANNAH. Yes, and the most mournful cries...You know that sound like someone in the most pure T. agony**...Like that time, Mama, you pulled my eyeteeth out and...

POE *(crosses R)*. This is ludicrous. The girl is lame. *(HANNAH starts to cry on MRS. O'LEARY's shoulder.)*

INSPECTOR GRIMKE *(crosses to POE)*. Sir, something suspicious has taken place on these premises and we mean to sort it out. Now, you and an acquaintance came in around midnight...*(POE turns his back on GRIMKE and refuses to answer. GRIMKE turns back to MRS. O'LEARY.)*...is that right, Mrs. O'Leary?

MRS. O'LEARY. Midnight or thereabouts...

* *"Light wood." Pronounced "lytard." Southern U.S. Pine wood, often of the Georgia pine. Any dry wood that burns readily.*
**An *idiom meaning "really bad."*

INSPECTOR GRIMKE *(wanders toward MRS. O'LEARY)*. ...There were angry words, words that led to an altercation perhaps...and now the gentleman in question is missing.

CONSTABLE ROSS *(crosses to POE)*. And we'd like to know his whereabouts.

POE *(crosses to ROSS)*. There was no gentle—oh, you think I've done away with him? Is that it...*(Stops.)*...wait a minute, this is someone's idea of a little fun, isn't it?

MRS. O'LEARY. It's certainly not my idea of a little fun.

POE *(faces GRIMKE)*. This is one of my stories you're acting out. Clever. *(Crosses C between ROSS and GRIMKE.)* Now I see. I had a little too much to drink and someone wanted to play a trick on me, brought me here—*(Motioning to the LADIES.)* and engaged you people to act this out...you're very good, you must be actors...

MRS. O'LEARY. Actors...I don't associate with that sort of riffraff...

POE *(to GRIMKE and ROSS)*. Who employed you? Mrs. O'Leary? Nimrod? Yes...Nimrod! *(Crosses to ROSS.)* He must have been angry with me, *(To GRIMKE.)* I wasn't on my best behavior last night, I'll admit. *(To ROSS.)* So Nimrod put you all up to this...quite clever having you act out *The Telltale Heart*.

CONSTABLE GRIMKE. Telltale heart?

POE *(a step toward ROSS)*. Are you going to pretend you've never heard of Edgar Allan Poe's *The Telltale Heart*?

MRS. O'LEARY *(a step toward GRIMKE)*. He told me his name was O'Quinn.

POE *(crosses to MRS. O'LEARY. She backs away a step)*. Madam, I never told you anything of the kind.

MRS. O'LEARY *(a step forward)*. If anyone's an actor, it's him, officer...

POE *(crosses to C between GRIMKE and ROSS)*. Let's all stop acting, shall we...I don't know what's going on here. Let's end this charade. *(POE alone begins to hear it, the low, quiet but unmistakable sound of a beating heart.)* Oh! You even have the sound...

INSPECTOR GRIMKE *(step toward POE)*. Sound?

POE *(crosses to GRIMKE)*. The heart...What is it...a clock? What did you do, muffle it to sound like a heart? *(Crosses to ROSS.)* Sounds pretty authentic.

MRS. O'LEARY *(whispering over GRIMKE's shoulder)*. The man is mad.

POE *(crosses DR)*. Where is it? *(He begins to search the room. ROSS goes to stop POE but GRIMKE holds up his hand as if to say, "No, wait." POE faces ROSS.)* The rug...under the rug...*(Crosses to DR. He starts for the rug, HANNAH steps back. POE throws the rug aside. GRIMKE crosses L and LADIES move toward C.)* Under a floorboard, right...*(The sound is almost overpowering. POE crosses to C.)* Here...no...over there...

MRS. O'LEARY. I had no idea I was letting to a madman...

POE *(kneels)*. Here...*(He pulls up the floorboard and reaches inside. He doesn't expect what he finds.)*

CONSTABLE ROSS. What is it? *(All move a step forward to see what's happening. In horror, POE pulls a bloody, beating heart from the floorboards. He rises, still holding the beating heart.)*

HANNAH *(back a step)*. Oh, my God...*(She throws herself into her mother's arms.)*

MRS. O'LEARY. Monster...

POE *(throwing the heart aside. Stands up)*. This has gone too far, gentlemen...

INSPECTOR GRIMKE *(crosses to POE)*. I think you better come with us...

POE. I'm not going anywhere until someone tells me what's going on...(*Crosses to GRIMKE.*) Where's the Captain?

CONSTABLE ROSS (*step toward POE*). There is no Captain here, sir. Now if you'll just come along with us.

POE (*crosses to ROSS*). Every ship has a Captain. I demand that you send for him. (*As he passes, MRS. O'LEARY and HANNAH cross L behind GRIMKE.*)

CONSTABLE ROSS. This isn't a ship, sir.

POE (*faces GRIMKE*). Of course it's a ship, bound for New York. Look, I'll end the charade. Just look out the port-hole. (*POE crosses UC to pull back the curtain on the porthole but when he does, the projection of porthole has vanished.*) This isn't amusing anymore. (*Starts L.*) I'm getting out of here.

MRS. O'LEARY. He's trying to escape...(*Backs up.*)

INSPECTOR GRIMKE (*steps in front of POE*). Halt!

CONSTABLE ROSS (*crosses and grabs POE by the arm*). Hold on, sir.

POE. Let me go. (*Throws ROSS to the floor R, then tries to exit. GRIMKE grabs him, they struggle.*)

MRS. O'LEARY. Stop him, stop him...(*HANNAH screams, and MRS. O'LEARY picks up one of Poe's stray [break-away] whiskey bottles and hits POE over the head with it. Delirious, POE falls to the floor. Lights tighten on him and others disappear into the darkness. The cry of the Raven is heard high above. In the darkness, the bed and table are quickly taken off and the U curtain rises to form a sail.*)

## SCENE 9: Are You All Right?

*On Deck*

*(Slowly the sounds of the sea are heard and POE awakens on deck.)*

RUSTY *(kneeling to the L of POE)*. Mr. Poe...

POE. What? Who?

RUSTY *(standing to the R of POE, he leans over)*. Are you all right?

POE. Oh, yes, I...*(He sits up. As he does, he rubs his head. He realizes his head is bleeding and wonders—was that a dream or reality that he just experienced?)*

RUSTY. He must have hit his head on the hatch during the storm.

MIGUEL. Sir, in bad weather you have to hold on and watch your head.

RUSTY. If you want to keep it.

POE *(staggers to his feet)*. Yes, I, must not have been watching where I was go—*(He stumbles, SAILORS catch him.)*

MIGUEL. I think you best sit and rest a bit. *(They sit him down on a small barrel DR.)*

RUSTY *(starts for the hatch UC)*. I'll get something for his head...

POE *(holding his handkerchief over the wound)*. No, it's just a scratch, I'm all right...

RUSTY *(stops, takes a step back toward POE)*. Are you sure, sir?

POE. Yes, yes...

MIGUEL. Can we get you anything...

POE. Perhaps something to drink...some spirits of some sort. *(MIGUEL doesn't want to give him more to drink, but he motions to RUSTY to exit for something to drink anyway. RUSTY exits D hatch in the apron.)*

MIGUEL. Yes, sir, of course...

POE. Thank you. *(MIGUEL crosses and squats beside POE, L. Takes out a cigar, offers one to POE, POE declines.)*

MIGUEL. You have to be careful on deck at night, sir. We wouldn't want to lose our most illustrious passenger... *(Stands, lights his cigar.)* What were you doing out here at this hour, anyway?

POE. I... ah...I had a most frightful dream and I suppose, I mean, I came up for some fresh air...

MIGUEL. Some storm we had. Must have awakened you. *(Crosses and throws his match off L.)*

POE. Yes, it did.

MIGUEL. Gave this old bucket a run for her money, it did, till we could strike some of the sails...*(Crosses back to POE.)* but don't worry, sir, she's a sound ship, and she's got an able crew, if I do say so myself.

POE. Yes, I can see that.

*(RUSTY returns from D hatch with a mug of rum. MI-GUEL and MIKE follow. They are wearing long rain capes and face U. MIKE kneels L of POE, MIGUEL to the R.)*

RUSTY. Here you go, sir...

MIKE. Something to knock the night chill off.

POE. Rum...Thank you...*(He drinks heartily.)*

MIGUEL. The boys will look after you, sir...If you'll excuse me, Rusty and I have to get some sleep. I have the midnight watch.

POE. Yes, yes, thank you. *(JAKE and RUSTY exit D though the hatch.)*

MIGUEL. Better, sir?

POE. Yes, thank you.
MIKE. Good.

*(POE drinks heartily again. Finishing his drink he brings his head forward and utters a sigh of relief but at that instant, the Raven cries again. POE looks up to it in terror and is instantly transformed into another nightmare:* The Masque of the Red Death. *Suddenly one of the sails unfurls to become a medieval tapestry. Music begins, MIKE and MIGUEL rise and turn around and as they do we see for the first time that they are dressed in medieval costumes. They twirl their capes, the inside of which are beautifully colored. MINSTRELS, JUGGLERS, TUMBLERS, etc., appear. Revelry ensues.)*

### SCENE 10: Masque of the Red Death

*Prince Prospero's Castle*

*(POE finds himself no longer on deck but far away, in a distant Medieval time and place. GUESTS wear grotesque masks.)*

VISCOUNT VALEQUEZ *(approaches POE).* Oh, what a strange costume...

POE. Costume?

DUCHESS ULRICA *(approaches POE).* Ooooooooo, I like it. I wager it will amuse the Prince...and we like to amuse our benefactor around here.

VISCOUNT VALEQUEZ *(who has approached them).* Benefactor? We're like rats in here...

DUCHESS ULRICA *(crosses to a banquet table to eat).* How can you say that? The Prince has marshaled his resources to build a wall between us and the plague which rages outside the gates.

VISCOUNT VALEQUEZ. He has put us in a cage and welded the gate shut. No one can come in and no one can go out. There is no means of ingress of egress...

DUCHESS ULRICA. Why would anyone want to go out? *(To POE.)* Really, the man complains about everything...I for one am glad the gates are welded shut. Keeps the rabble and their filthy disease outside. *(Crosses to get a goblet of wine from a passing pageboy.)*

POE *(realizing where he is).* The Red Death.

VISCOUNT VALEQUEZ. Yes, the Red Death...no pestilence has ever been so fatal, or so hideous. "Blood its avatar and its seal..."

DUCHESS ULRICA *(turns back to VISCOUNT).* Don't glorify the Red Death, my dear Viscount, you make it sound like royalty.

VISCOUNT VALEQUEZ. And why not? It gets more attention these days than the Prince himself. *(He gets wine from the pageboy, then turns to POE.)* I, for one, would give anything to get out of here.

DUCHESS ULRICA *(motioning to all the entertainers and food about).* Are you mad? We are well provisioned here and the Prince has provided all the appliances of pleasure. There are jugglers, minstrels, improvvisatori, buffoons...

VISCOUNT VALEQUEZ *(crosses to DUCHESS).* And the only thing that make it palatable is the fact that it is rumored that the Prince has the finest cellar in all of Europe...and just to be sure, the Viscount there plans to sample every bottle...*(Lifts his glass.)* Yes, my dear—To the Red Death who has given us this oasis of ostentation.

DUCHESS ULRICA *(crosses to VISCOUNT)*. Must you be so morbid, Viscount? *(To POE.)* We came here to seek shelter from the Red Death and that's all anyone talks about. Well, I, for one, have left it behind. *(Crosses L past POE.)*

VISCOUNT VALEQUEZ. No one leaves it behind. *(He drinks again.)* You must be one of the new ones.

POE. Yes, I just arrived.

VISCOUNT VALEQUEZ. How did you get to be so lucky?

POE. Lucky?

VISCOUNT VALEQUEZ. To be given sanctuary here, till the Red Death goes away?

POE. If it goes away.

VISCOUNT VALEQUEZ. Ooooh, I like you...*(A fanfare sounds.)*

DUCHESS ULRICA. The Prince! *(She flutters off to make a good impression.)*

VISCOUNT VALEQUEZ. Our illustrious benefactor. Perhaps someone is clever enough to outwit the Red Death, but I hardly think it will be our brilliant Prince there.

POE. Why not?

VISCOUNT VALEQUEZ. Look at him.

*(PRINCE PROSPERO enters, dressed in ostentatious silliness, a wreath of fruit on his head, and LADY PROSPERO by his side. They cross UC.)*

VISCOUNT VALEQUEZ. He's a buffoon.

POE. You don't like him.

VISCOUNT VALEQUEZ. No.

POE. Any particular reason?

VISCOUNT VALEQUEZ. A mere accident of birth. He was born first.

POE. So, you might have been Prince.

VISCOUNT VALEQUEZ. Might have been...That's a plague in itself...

PRINCE PROSPERO. My dear friends, for tonight's amusement, I've composed a little epic trifle of a poem...

VISCOUNT VALEQUEZ. Here we go. I can't wait to see his face when he comes face to face with the Red Death.

POE. You think the Red Death will penetrate the high walls about the castle?

VISCOUNT VALEQUEZ. My dear boy, I'm counting on it.

PRINCE PROSPERO *(recites)*.

Again we gather in this hall of mirth

Tipping our tumblers, improving our girth

Our neverending feast may it never end

And if it does, may it begin again

As Prince of this realm I proclaim, Don't be wary,

Let the jesters jest, Let the Merry be Merry! *(There is an explosion of frivolity.)*

DUCHESS ULRICA *(as PRINCE and his entourage pass by)*. Your Highness, what moving verses, I hardly know how to express—

PRINCE PROSPERO *(raising his hand)*. Silence...

DUCHESS ULRICA. Your Highness, I—*(The PRINCE raises his hand, again. He crosses DR toward POE. The DUCH-ESS makes a deep curtsy, as do others. MEN, except POE, bow and remove their hats. The PRINCE turns to an attendant.)*

LADY PROSPERO. Who is that?

PRINCE PROSPERO. I do not know, my dear...a stranger...

LADY PROSPERO *(indignant)*. There are not supposed to be any strangers here.

VISCOUNT VALEQUEZ *(a step forward)*. A friend of mine, dear brother.

PRINCE PROSPERO. You know the rules, no strangers here. Do you want to endanger us all?

VISCOUNT VALEQUEZ. A thousand apologies.

PRINCE PROSPERO. And you could at least teach him some manners.

VISCOUNT VALEQUEZ *(to POE)*. Remove your hat, dear boy.

POE. What?

VISCOUNT VALEQUEZ. Your hat, you must remove it in the presence of the Prince. *(POE removes his hat and exposes a bandage that is bloodied.)*

DUCHESS ULRICA *(shrinking away)*. Ah...the Red Death... *(POE is puzzled, then realizes there is a bloody bandage on his head, apparently from the bottle that hit him in the preceding nightmare.)*

VISCOUNT VALEQUEZ. It's only a costume...he's come to the masque in the costume of one with the Red Death... How clever. *(All laugh nervously, a few murmur in approval or disapproval.)*

DUCHESS ULRICA *(angry, poking her husband to do something)*. Too clever.

PRINCE PROSPERO *(furious with rage)*. How dare you insult us with this blasphemous mockery. Seize him and unmask him that we may know who to hang at sunrise. *(No one moves. Guards shrink away, fearful of the Red Death.)* Seize him, I say! Seize him...*(Still no one moves.)* Must I seize him myself? *(Reaching up for POE's bandage.)* Take off that ridiculous costume...

POE. No, please...

PRINCE PROSPERO. Take it off...you think you can frighten us with that masquerade? I warn you not to trifle with the power of a Prince, not Prince Prospero...*(As he grabs the bandage, he pulls it off.)* Ah...*(He looks at his hand, it is covered with blood—real blood.)* It's real...

DUCHESS ULRICA *(in horror).* The Red Death is here...

LADY PROSPERO. You said you could lock it out...you promised...

PRINCE PROSPERO. My dear...*(Unthinkingly, he touches her cheek to comfort her, but smears her cheek with blood.)*

LADY PROSPERO. Fool! Look what you've done. Look what you've done! *(She grabs her cheek, wiping the blood from it—then shakes her hand to get the blood off of her. The blood hits other members of the crowd who begin to scream. The sail curtains fall and the writhing crowds become silhouettes of red light. They begin to sink to the floor in agony. Soon, all except POE writhe and fall dead to the floor.)*

POE *(crosses to them).* Very funny...very funny...You can get up now. Get up...

*(From out of the D trap, a hooded figure dressed in a death masque appears. He crosses to POE. He removes his mask and we see that it is NIMROD.)*

### SCENE 11: Are You Death?

*Prince Prospero's Castle*

POE. Nimrod. *(The Raven cries above. NIMROD looks up to it.)*

CAPTAIN NIMROD. Yes, yes. Don't be impatient, my pet.

POE. You can hear him?

CAPTAIN NIMROD. Of course.

POE. You're in league with the devil.

CAPTAIN NIMROD *(with a laugh).* Oh, no, my dear boy...I *am* the devil...although I'm not very fond of that *nom-de-plume*...Sounds so childish, don't you think?...I much prefer Lucifer—has a ring to it, don't you think?...Lucifer, just rolls off your tongue, like a poem. Of course, I'd value your opinion on the subject. You're the poet after all...*(He removes his hood.)*

POE. Am I in hell? Have I...

CAPTAIN NIMROD. Crossed over...passed on?

POE. Died?

CAPTAIN NIMROD *(smiles, then:).* The boundaries which divide life from death are at best shadowy and vague. Who shall say where the one ends and the other begins?

POE. Why are you subjecting me to these nightmares?

CAPTAIN NIMROD. Well, they are your nightmares, after all.

POE. Why have you brought me here?

CAPTAIN NIMROD. I?...You are here of your own volition, Edgar...You have reached out to the dark forces of the universe and we have simply welcomed your embrace...You got what you wanted, a grand literary career. It's a pity you didn't ask for a fortune to go with your fame. It could easily have been part of the bargain.

POE. Bargain?...

CAPTAIN NIMROD. My feathered friend tells me you've been a bit remiss about paying up...But take your time, my boy. Of course, the longer you wait, the more unpleasant it will become...

POE. What do you mean—unpleasant?

CAPTAIN NIMROD. Well, you see, until you agree to cross over and join us, you shall continue to live in the worlds you have imagined...going from story to story and some of them, I believe, are quite unpleasant...So if I were you, I would get this over with, submit...I can assure you that you will receive a hero's welcome...After all, you've made our dark world quite renowned...

POE. That was not my intention...

CAPTAIN NIMROD. No, your intention was to make yourself renowned, wasn't it...Well, you got that, didn't you?

POE. I won't submit...

CAPTAIN NIMROD. Then your nightmares will continue...

*(Two large, dark-hooded FIGURES appear.)*

POE. Until...

CAPTAIN NIMROD. Until you are persuaded...*(Motions to the two FIGURES who cross toward POE.)* And believe me, we're very good at persuasion...*(The Raven cries, the dark FIGURES grab POE. NIMROD disappears. Lightning and thunder crash. Wind builds. POE struggles. The curtains rise to form folded curtains again and we are once more on the ship.)*

### SCENE 12: The Oblong Box

*The Ship*

*(POE is transported back to the ship. A violent storm is underway. POE looks to his arms and realizes they are being held by MIKE and RUSTY, their figures having been hidden by dark rain cloaks.)*

POE. Let me go, let me go...*(They release him.)*

RUSTY. We were only trying to steady you, sir.

POE. Steady me?

MIKE. Sorry, the sea is a bit rough tonight, sir...

RUSTY. Not a good night to be out on deck...

MIKE. Our apologies...

RUSTY. Would you like us to help you below, sir?

POE. No...get away...

*(REYNOLDS comes from below with NIMROD.)*

REYNOLDS. Edgar...what's wrong here?

RUSTY. I think he's had a bit too much to drink, sir.

POE. Too much to—No. *(Grabs REYNOLDS and pulls him aside.)* They're agents of the devil.

CAPTAIN NIMROD. My crew?

POE. And he's their Captain, the devil himself!

REYNOLDS. Edgar.

POE. They're all after me...

REYNOLDS. But, my dear fellow...

POE. They want my soul...

REYNOLDS. Your soul? *(The cry of the Raven is heard.)*

POE. You hear, the raven up there, like an albatross circling, laughing at me...the Captain's in league with him.

REYNOLDS. Edgar, it's only a sea bird...and the Captain—

POE. We must escape...We must escape! There is no time to lose...We must get off this ship!

REYNOLDS. Edgar, but we are at sea. If I may be so bold...you have had quite a bit to drink tonight...I think perhaps you drifted off to sleep and your imagination, which everyone knows is quite vivid, went to work on you...

POE. You think I was dreaming?

REYNOLDS. No doubt...

POE. I did sleep, but when I did, I awoke inside my own stories...

REYNOLDS. You see...you were still dreaming...

POE. No, look.

REYNOLDS. What?

POE. Don't you see?

REYNOLDS. What?

POE. The box. *(He notices an oblong box which, in this scene, has appeared on deck for the first time.)*

REYNOLDS. What about it?

POE. It's the oblong box...

REYNOLDS. You mean from your story?

POE. Yes, it portends disaster.

REYNOLDS. Disaster?

POE. Don't you remember?...In the story...the box contained the body of a young woman...and a dead body is bad luck on a ship...and the ship sank in a storm off Ocracoke.

REYNOLDS. This is not one of your stories, Edgar.

POE. We must throw it overboard.

REYNOLDS. Edgar, please...

CAPTAIN NIMROD. Stop him...*(SAILORS grab his arm, POE pushes them away and begins to grapple with the crate.)*

POE. Let me go...It's an omen...It will spell our doom...

REYNOLDS. Edgar, listen to me...

POE. Why should I listen to you? I don't even know if you are real?...You may be just a character in one of my stories, too.

CAPTAIN NIMROD. Mr. Poe, you are not well, you must desist...

POE. No, you'll see, you'll see...this oblong box contains a corpse, we must cast it overboard...*(A struggle ensues and the oblong box is overturned. Its lid falls open and the box is found to be empty.)* Empty...

CAPTAIN NIMROD. Mr. Poe, I really must insist you not tamper with our cargo...*(The box is righted and the lid is closed.)*

POE. What have you done with it?

JAKE. What, sir?

POE. The corpse. *(To REYNOLDS, as the SAILORS begin to mumble among themselves about the loon they have on board.)* Don't you see...He's spirited it away in a effort to make me look...Perhaps I am...*(He crosses apart from the others a bit, then asks:)* Dear God, give me sign that I am not mad...

REYNOLDS. Edgar, it's just a coincidence. The box reminded you of one of your stories. *(Annabel's theme is heard.)*

POE. Coincidence?

*(Mysteriously and slowly, there rises from the box a VISION IN WHITE... POE sees it... The others don't.)*

POE. No, look...

REYNOLDS. What?

POE. Don't you see her?

CAPTAIN NIMROD. Her?

REYNOLDS. Who?

POE. The corpse, there...She's arisen from the box!

REYNOLDS. Eddie, we see no one. *(POE looks to the others and realizes no one sees what he sees.)*

POE *(grabbing REYNOLDS).* You must...*(Sadly REYNOLDS shakes his head "no." The VISION turns around.)* My God, it's Annabel...

CAPTAIN NIMROD. Annabel?

POE. My first love...the truest love I've ever known...

REYNOLDS. And you think you see her?

POE. Yes...there...Annabel...

ANNABEL. I'm here, Eddie...

POE. She speaks...

CAPTAIN NIMROD. And what does she say?

POE. She speaks, but I cannot hear her...

CAPTAIN NIMROD. Isn't that a shame?

POE *(doubting what he's seen)*. What's happening to me, Jeremiah?

REYNOLDS. Your imagination's gotten the best of you.

CAPTAIN NIMROD. Let us help you below, sir...

POE. Yes, yes...

CAPTAIN NIMROD. Help him to his cabin.

SAILOR. Yes, sir. *(They take him below.)*

REYNOLDS. I'll look after him.

CAPTAIN NIMROD. Yes, you do that. *(They exit. NIMROD goes as if to follow them and for a moment, we think he hasn't seen ANNABEL either, but he stops near the hatch and turns back to her.)* Nice try, my dear, but as you can see, he didn't even believe his own eyes. So off with you. You know the dominions of heaven have no power here.

ANNABEL. I know that.

CAPTAIN NIMROD. You will only prolong his agony, go back to your kingdom of glory.

ANNABEL. What will it take to win him a reprieve?

CAPTAIN NIMROD. There are no reprieves here...he has sold his soul...it is ours now...the bargain is sealed.

ANNABEL. What about a new bargain?

CAPTAIN NIMROD. A new bargain?

ANNABEL. My soul for his.

CAPTAIN NIMROD. An even trade? There's nothing to be gained by that, my dear, although I must say, yours is one soul I would love to have won.

ANNABEL. Perhaps you can still win it.

CAPTAIN NIMROD. What do you mean?

ANNABEL. Give Eddie a chance to find his way out of your dark realm...to write again, without your help, from his own imagination, from his heart...

CAPTAIN NIMROD. And if he does?

ANNABEL. You release your hold on him.

CAPTAIN NIMROD. And if he fails...

ANNABEL. You get both our souls...

CAPTAIN NIMROD. I didn't realize your kind went in for wagers...

ANNABEL. Oh yes.

CAPTAIN NIMROD. You must especially like long shots...

ANNABEL. We specialize in them...

CAPTAIN NIMROD. Very well...we shall reach the gateway to the netherworld by dawn, I will give him till then...to write again of his own accord...but a few conditions...You may observe him, but you may not make yourself visible to him nor may you touch him...or speak to him...not a word.

ANNABEL. Until...

CAPTAIN NIMROD. Until of his own accord, he picks up his pen.

ANNABEL. Very well...and into the meantime...

CAPTAIN NIMROD. The voyage into darkness continues...
*(He waves his hand and the scene shifts.)*

## SCENE 13: The Gold Bug

*The Beach at Sullivans Island*

*(The sound of the ocean is heard. The D sail is lowered and shadows of palmetto trees are projected on it. Once again, POE is back on Sullivans Island. U and behind him, MR. LEGRAND rushes on-stage in a state of excitement. He's dragging POE with him.)*

LEGRAND *(over POE's shoulder)*. See, I want to show you what I found.

POE. Found? *(LEGRAND pours the contents of a small canvas bag he has been carrying onto the ground. Out pours a mound of sand, in the middle of which is something that glitters of gold. LEGRAND reaches down picks up the gold object and shows it to POE.)*

LEGRAND. Have you ever seen anything like it? Solid gold, every inch of him.

POE. *The Gold Bug...*

LEGRAND. And look at the back, see the two jet black spots...*(He hands it to POE.)*

POE *(without looking at it)*. Like a skull, a death head... *(Hands it back to LEGRAND.)*

LEGRAND *(taking it)*. Yes, rather like that, a skull and cross-bones...

POE. Perhaps left by pirates.

LEGRAND. Yes...that would make sense...perfect sense... and it would explain the parchment...See, I found this parchment in the sand near where I found the Gold Bug... You're right, it must be a pirate's treasure map. That would explain everything...Now if we can just decipher it, we can find the treasure...Just think, that the key to the pirate's treasure has lain buried here on Sullivans for over a hundred years...

POE. Sullivans...We're on Sullivans?

LEGRAND. Of course, did you think we were on the mainland?...See, once we crossed over the marsh, we were on Sullivans Island.

POE. Yes, I've been here before.

LEGRAND. When?

POE. Many years ago...

LEGRAND. What were you doing here?

POE. I was stationed at Ft. Moultrie.

LEGRAND. A soldier boy.

POE *(crosses D)*. A boy, a least...a child...*(Lights tighten in on him. LEGRAND disappears. POE wanders down the beach.)* "I was a child and she was a child...in this kingdom by the sea...and we loved with a love that was more than love...once, once...but that was long ago..." *(He falls on his knees on the beach.)* Oh, Annabel...I'm lost...lost in shadows of my own imagining...Were you there on deck for me, were you the sign I prayed for...or were you just a hollow hallucination...for I don't know what is real anymore...what is real and what isn't...I don't even know whether you were real...or whether I just imagined you or that even now, I'm just imagining that I imagined you...If only I could reach across the abyss and touch you once more...a touch to know that indeed you were real...if only...

*(His head drops; he weeps in despair. U, the sail curtains rise and ANNABEL, enveloped in fog, appears as if in a vision. She crosses to POE.)*

ANNABEL *(kneels beside him but he cannot see her)*. If only, Eddie...my hand is here...*(She holds out her hand.)* ...but it is you, Eddie, who must reach across the abyss...I cannot touch you...I cannot speak to you...but know that I am with you...*(She turns her hand over and a handful of sand falls on the ground, a bit of which touches POE's fingers. ANNABEL crosses back U into silhouette. As she does, POE's fingers touch the sand, play with it, caress it. After a moment, he is aware that it is there.)*

POE *(wonders: Could it be a sign from her?)*. Annabel?... *(But his doubts are stronger and he gives up.)* Annabel... *(Still he wonders.)* I stand amid the roar of a surf-tormented shore, and I hold within my hand grains of golden sand...How few...yet how they creep through my fingers to the deep, while I weep...while I weep...Oh, God! Can I not grasp them with a tighter clasp? Oh, God! Can I not save one from the pitiless wave? Is all that I see or seem but a dream within a dream? *(He holds his hand up, releasing the grains of sand. The sound of the ocean's roar rises and lights fade. The Raven cries.)*

CURTAIN—END OF ACT ONE

# ACT TWO

## SCENE 14: The Predicament

*Poe's Bed. Clock Steeple*

*(As the Raven cries again, lights crossfade to POE lying in his bed. Poe's bed, however, is seen high in the air at a very sharp angle to the stage. It appears as if we're high overhead looking down on the bed. Lighting is very tight here and all we can see is POE, his bedspread and a pillow. In the distance a church bell is striking the hour. POE awakens with a start.)*

POE. A dream...it's all a dream...yes...yes...a dream...

*(The church bell strikes again, this time with a deafening sound. POE is startled again and throws off the bedspread. As he does, black curtains, which have hidden the clock, fly out and lights broaden in the scene to reveal that he is not in bed at all. Instead he is high on a church steeple, leaning precariously against the church clock. We hear, growing in intensity, the sound of the clock mechanism, ticking, turning, and note to our horror that the huge minute hand is slowly pushing POE over the edge. He is pushed closer and closer to the edge. The cry of the Raven is heard. POE looks up to it. CAPTAIN NIMROD appears at the opposite ledge of the clock.)*

CAPTAIN NIMROD. *Tempus fugit?*

POE. Nimrod!

CAPTAIN NIMROD. Oh, I like this story.

POE. *The Predicament.*

CAPTAIN NIMROD. Such an appropriate title, don't you think, considering it is such a long way down? But don't worry, the hands of the clock won't cut off your head as they do in your story. I thought that was a bit too macabre, even for you. There is such a finality about that. Besides, it would spoil all the fun.

POE. So, I'll be pushed off the ledge instead.

CAPTAIN NIMROD. Time will tell, my friend...Time will tell.

POE. You may have purchased my soul—lock, stock and barrel—but I am not your friend...nor will I ever be.

CAPTAIN NIMROD. Pity...I thought perhaps by now, you'd be ready to give up your futile struggle.

POE. Never.

CAPTAIN NIMROD. Never...Where have I heard that before? *(He motions and the minute hand moves a bit, pushing POE closer to the edge.)*

POE. Why do you torture me like this?

CAPTAIN NIMROD. Torture? This isn't torture. This is a mere amusement...

POE. Well, I'm not very amused...*(The Raven crises, laughingly.)*

CAPTAIN NIMROD *(indicating the Raven)*. The Raven is... *(The Raven cries again. NIMROD disappears.)*

POE. Laugh then...laugh if you will. You find it amusing that I find myself here in a predicament of my own devising... trapped here on a ledge of the imagination...dangling between heaven and hell...Will you give me no respite?...No mercy? *(The Raven cries laughingly.)*...Laugh then... laugh...fiend...villain...laaaaaaaaaaaaaaaugh...(The minute *hand pushes him off and he falls into the fog-covered area below.)*

**SCENE 15: The Fall**

*On the Deck of the Ship*

*(CABIN BOYS rush on-stage from UC. D, POE lies prostrate on the deck. Several SAILORS have gathered around him. They are murmuring.)*

CABIN BOYS. He's right up here, sir.

*(REYNOLDS enters.)*

REYNOLDS. Edgar, no...

*(CAPTAIN NIMROD rushes in.)*

CAPTAIN NIMROD. What happened?

JAKE. He fell from the mainsail rigging, sir...Rusty saw it.

RUSTY. We looked up and there he was, ranting and raving about heaven and hell or something...Miguel lit out up the ladder for him but before he could get there he lost his grip and...

MIGUEL. He didn't lose his grip, he jumped...

REYNOLDS. Jumped...

MIGUEL. I reached out my hand to him but he was terrified of me, of all of us. He jumped to get away from us.

POE *(awakening)*. Ahhh...

REYNOLDS. Edgar...

CAPTAIN NIMROD. Get some water...*(CABIN BOY 1 exits for a bucket of water.*

POE. Jeremiah...is that you?

REYNOLDS. You've had a fall...

POE. A fall...no, I was pushed...pushed from the church steeple...the hands of the clock pushed me off the ledge.

REYNOLDS. Clock? There is no clock, Edgar...

CAPTAIN NIMROD. You fell from the rigging...*(REYNOLDS nods his head "yes.")*

POE. He's bewitched you...don't you see?

REYNOLDS. Who...

POE *(pulling REYNOLDS down to him)*. The Captain...you see only what he wants you to see...

REYNOLDS. Edgar, really.

POE. ...Please, please you must believe me, Jeremiah... you're my only hope...Please get me off this vessel...

REYNOLDS. When we reach our destination in the morning, I'll get you ashore first thing...

POE *(desperate)*. Promise me.

*(CABIN BOY 1 enters.)*

CABIN BOY 1. Drink, sir?

REYNOLDS. I promise...Rest now...rest and regain your strength...

POE. You're a good friend, Jeremiah, a good friend...*(He loses consciousness.)*

CAPTAIN NIMROD *(to the CREWMEN)*. Take him to his cabin...and secure him to his bunk. We don't want any more wandering about.

REYNOLDS. Well, Captain, I'd say you have him...

CAPTAIN NIMROD. He's a tough one, but with a little more persuasion he'll come around. I must say, you play your part very well...

CAPTAIN REYNOLDS. I want to earn my keep.

CAPTAIN NIMROD. And you have. Jeremiah, you have... *(He puts his arm around REYNOLDS, who then exits. The Raven cries, NIMROD stops, looks up at Raven.)* Patience, my pet, patience. *(Lights fade. The U curtain falls and POE's bed is brought on and placed at C, as in Scene 8.)*


## SCENE 16: The Pit and the Pendulum

*(A tight spot rises on POE, lying prone in his bunk.)*

POE. Another awakening...is this yet another dream or reality...

*(Suddenly from overhead the fabled scythed pendulum swings in. POE must recoil so it doesn't hit his head. He struggles but realizes he is chained to the platform. The pendulum swings, lower and lower. As it is about to make its final pass it disappears offstage and when it returns, it is not the pendulum at all, but a hanging lantern, the lantern in Poe's cabin. REYNOLDS enters.)*

REYNOLDS. Feeling better?

POE. Jeremiah, thank God, you've broken the spell...

REYNOLDS. Spell?

POE. The pendulum was swinging overhead, growing closer and closer...

REYNOLDS. It's only a lantern, Eddie, swaying with the ship...*(He reaches up and steadies the lantern.)*

POE. No, it was the pendulum.

REYNOLDS. Like your story!

POE. Yes! And I was bound here beneath it.

REYNOLDS. You were bound here to keep you from wandering about in your inebriated condition.

POE. Untie me!

REYNOLDS. If you promise to stay below. It's rough up on deck.

POE. All right, all right...

REYNOLDS. But there is good news. Since the wind has picked up, we shall reach our destination by dawn.

POE. And then you'll get me off this phantom ship.

REYNOLDS. I promised, didn't I?...

POE. Well, when we reach New York...

REYNOLDS. We won't reach New York, Edgar.

POE. What do you mean? You said, we'd reach our destination at dawn...

REYNOLDS. And we shall...but it's not New York.

POE. I don't understand...

REYNOLDS. We have a new destination...I told you I had a new adventure to share with you...

POE. Where are we bound?

REYNOLDS. We are bound, Edgar, for the Antarctic... *(Music plays. The U sail rises to expose the bow of the ship, now ice-covered. Off the bow is a giant iceberg. In the distance are seen swirling reflections coming from the maelstrom.)*

POE. How could we be in the Antarctic after only one day at sea?

REYNOLDS *(crosses to POE)*. The powers here, Edgar, defy the imagination...

POE. The powers here? My God, you're part of this, too...
part of this horrible nightmare...How could you lead me
on like this?...Where have you brought me?

REYNOLDS *(up on the bow)*. To the edge of earthly exis-
tence...And there, ahead—the Gateway to Hell itself,
Edgar. I came upon it on my last voyage...Beautiful, isn't
it? A giant swirling vortex...descending into the nether-
world...

POE *(fascinated. Crosses to REYNOLDS)*. The Maelstrom!

REYNOLDS. Yes, I knew, if anyone, you would appreciate
my discovery.

POE *(repulsed and attracted at the same time)*. It's horrify-
ing...(*POE shivers from the cold, cold that does not seem
to affect REYNOLDS.*)

REYNOLDS. Yes, isn't it? I knew the moment I saw it that
you were the person to chronicle my greatest discovery. Of
course, the only problem was that no one had ever escaped
the swirling grip of the Maelstrom.

POE. Then how did you escape?

REYNOLDS. I made special arrangements.

POE. With whom? *(Then it dawns on him.)* You sold your
soul!

REYNOLDS *(waves his hand and the U sail flies back in)*. It
wasn't such a bad bargain...I got a chance to return to the
land of the living and the chance to appear in the world's
greatest mystery story.

POE. Written by me.

REYNOLDS. Of course.

POE. The story Nimrod wanted me to write...You're doing
his bidding for him! Why, Jeremiah? Why? What has he
promised you? What could implore you to—The chance to
walk among the living again...That's what he offered you,
isn't it? To release his hold on you...in exchange for what?

*(REYNOLDS is silent.)* You, you've crossed over...you've sold your soul? *(The U sail curtain slowly falls and when it is down, actors playing characters from Poe's stories get in place behind it.)*

REYNOLDS. Don't judge me too harshly, Eddie...You must consider the circumstances. Nimrod offered to save my ship...if, if I would help bring you here.

POE. You saved your soul by serving up my head on a silver platter...

REYNOLDS. I had no choice, Eddie...

POE. We all have choices, Jeremiah...


*(NIMROD enters.)*


CAPTAIN NIMROD. Spare yourself the agony, Edgar.

REYNOLDS. Listen to Nimrod, he will persuade you.

POE. And if I refuse to be persuaded?

REYNOLDS. Don't, Edgar. The horrors are too great...besides, all your friends are here. *(He takes a book out of his pocket.)*

POE. Friends?...*(REYNOLDS hands the book to NIMROD who opens it and reads. As he does, the Poe CHARACTERS he describes appear.)*

CAPTAIN NIMROD. Yes. "Extraordinary Murders—This morning, about three o'clock, the inhabitants were roused by a succession of terrific shrieks issuing from the fourth story of a house in the Rue Morgue, known to be the sole occupancy of one..."


*(Lights rise U of the U sail curtain creating a giant silhouette of MADAME L'ESPANAYE and her daughter, MADEMOISELLE CAMILLE L'ESPANAYE.)*

MME. L'ESPANAYE. Madame L'Espanaye...*(She curtsies.)*
CAPTAIN NIMROD. And her daughter...
MLLE. CAMILLE L'ESPANAYE. Mademoiselle Camille L'Espanaye...*(She, too, curtsies.)*
CAPTAIN NIMROD *(picks up another manuscript and reads).* "A letter, highly agitated in nature, lately reached me—summoned me to visit my old friend...signed in a nervous script was the name..."

*(The silhouette of RODERICK USHER appears.)*

RODERICK USHER. Roderick Usher...*(Bows.)*
POE. Usher...*The House of Usher...*
CAPTAIN NIMROD *(grabs up another manuscript page and reads).* Ah, my favorite. He was a professional jester and dwarf. His name was conferred on him on account of his inability to walk as other men...
POE. Hopfrog...

*(HOPFROG's silhouette appears.)*

HOPFROG. Hello, Eddie...
POE. What are you doing here?
MME. L'ESPANAYE. We are all here...*(The cry of the Raven is heard.)*
REYNOLDS *(as other figures appear from the shadows).* All your creations...
CAPTAIN NIMROD. Quite a *dramatis personae*, wouldn't you agree?
POE. And to what honor do I owe the performance of this cosmic repertory company?...
MLLE. CAMILLE L'ESPANAYE. You have given us immortal life...

RODERICK USHER. And we want to return the favor. *(HOPFROG stifles a giggle.)*

MME. L'ESPANAYE. The only question is how to do it?

RODERICK USHER. Suffocation...

MLLE. L'ESPANAYE. Drowning...

HOPFROG. Decapitation?

MME. L'ESPANAYE. Something exotic? Murder at the hands of an orangutan, perhaps...*(HOPFROG snickers again. POE steps back a few paces.)*

CAPTAIN NIMROD. You're not frightened are you, Eddie? Not you of all people?

POE. I created you, all of you. How can you turn on me?

RODERICK USHER. We're not turning on you.

MLLE. L'ESPANAYE. We simply want you to join us...

POE. In hell?

HOPFROG. What's wrong with hell?

CAPTAIN NIMROD. Yes, a little late to get squeamish about purgatory, Edgar...

POE. Just because I wrote about the dark side of human nature doesn't mean I want to embrace it...

HOPFROG. Oh, please, next he'll be telling us he's an angel at heart. *(All laugh.)*

POE. No, I am no angel but...some men choose to live in the shadows and others have shadows cast over them...

MME. L'ESPANAYE. By what?

POE. Circumstances...

MME. L'ESPANAYE *(looking to the others, she smiles).* Circumstances...

CAPTAIN NIMROD *(with a touch of triumph).* Not the master of your soul, Edgar?

POE. I'm surrounded by characters of my own creation who are about to murder me...How can I be the master of my soul?

REYNOLDS. Exactly...You've fought a good fight but it's time to surrender...to the circumstances...

POE. And if I don't...

HOPFROG *(annoyed)*. Oh, please...

POE *(forcefully to REYNOLDS)*. And if I don't...

REYNOLDS. You will live in your nightmares...

POE. For how long?

CAPTAIN NIMROD. *Ad infinitum...*

POE *(desperate, becoming overwhelmed by the madness)*. I don't believe you...Everyone must wake up from their nightmares sooner or later.

CAPTAIN NIMROD. Must they?

POE *(approaching delirium, falls to his knees)*. Yes...there must be a way. I just, just have to find it...

REYNOLDS. People like us belong here, Edgar... It's our destiny...Give in...give in. *(POE kneels there silently and for a moment, we think that perhaps he will. NIMROD and REYNOLDS look at each other in triumph.)*

POE. I must find a way...It's out there...I know it...If I could only touch it...

*(POE reaches out his hand. Annabel's theme is heard and her shadow appears U.)*

CAPTAIN NIMROD. There is nothing you can do for him...

REYNOLDS. He's ours...

ANNABEL. He still holds on...

REYNOLDS. Only by a thread...

CAPTAIN NIMROD. Speak to him...and both your souls are mine...

ANNABEL. I know the rules...*(She waves her hand and pages and pages of paper fall from above the stage.)* No rule can contain the imagination.

POE. What's this?

REYNOLDS. Another nightmare, Edgar? They will go on and on until you give in...

POE (*picking up the pages*). Blank...these pages are blank...

REYNOLDS. There's no greater terror, you said once.

POE. Yes...(*Remembering the pages ANNABEL gave him long ago.*)...but...once I delighted in empty pages... pages...pages...to be filled with wonder...These are from Annabel...aren't they?

REYNOLDS. Don't be ridiculous.

POE. She's trying to tell me something...something you won't tell me.

CAPTAIN NIMROD. Now what wouldn't we tell you, Edgar?

POE. That there is a way out of this nightmare...

REYNOLDS. There is...surrender.

POE. These pages are hope...My soul isn't lost, is it? There is still a chance for redemption...

CAPTAIN NIMROD. Redemption is not a word we use here.

POE. No, I imagine not. That would be your hell, wouldn't it, having someone slip through your clutches?

CAPTAIN NIMROD. Very few do...

POE. But there are a few, aren't there? (*NIMROD refuses to answer.*) Aren't there?

CAPTAIN NIMROD (*begrudgingly*). Yes...

REYNOLDS. But most, Edgar, perish in trying. Believe me, you can't imagine the agonies.

POE. Then perhaps I shall imagine something else...If all these nightmares have come from my tales of terror, perhaps it's time to write a new tale...a tale of redemption...

CAPTAIN NIMROD. Writing, I believe, requires more than a blank sheet of paper...You are clever, my boy, but not quite clever enough. You have paper but no pen? (*POE removes a pen from his pocket and smiles.)* And ink? *(POE searches but knows he has no ink. NIMROD gloats to REYNOLDS.)* Ah, what's this, no ink?

REYNOLDS. A pity. *(They chuckle. While they do so, POE takes a penknife, slashes his wrist.)* The man's slashed his wrist! *(POE then uses his own blood to write his story. As he begins to write NIMROD and REYNOLDS race to stop him.)*

REYNOLDS/CAPTAIN NIMROD. Noooooooooooooo...

REYNOLDS. Noooooooooooo...*(POE writes. As he does, NIMROD and REYNOLDS are thwarted. The silhouettes of Poe's characters fade away and the D sail curtain falls in front of NIMROD and REYNOLDS. POE is left alone, D, writing his way out of his nightmare.)*

POE. The phantoms faded away as the ship entered the harbor. I recognized it at once, the spires of St. Philip's and St. Michael's looming across the mists...Charleston...*(He stops writing and looks out over the harbor.)* A cryptic note had summoned me there...on most urgent business, the letter said. It led me to a fashionable part of the city in the middle of which was a large mansion, the worse for wear...I made my way to the massive heart pine door, brushed the cobwebs from the tarnished brass knocker and knocked...No one answered...but in the gentle breeze that blew, I noticed the window curtains dancing at the French doors which were open onto the piazza...I made my way through them and wandered inside...the house appeared long since abandoned...*(The D curtain rises to reveal the dust-covered furniture in the room.)*...furniture covered in dust covers...I wondered if it was all a charade, another cruel trick played on me...

## SCENE 17: Hello, Eddie

*The Drawing Room*

*(ANNABEL LEE appears beneath one of the dust covers on one of the tall pieces of furniture, the dust cover becoming a white cape.)*

ANNABEL. Hello, Eddie...

POE. Annabel?

ANNABEL. I haven't grown so old that you don't recognize me?

POE. No, you're lovely, but...

ANNABEL. Oh, Eddie, such a cruel hoax was played on you.

POE. Hoax?

ANNABEL. My death...all a cruel deception, I'm afraid.

POE. I don't understand...I thought the fever...

ANNABEL. The fever passed, then...

POE. But why didn't I know? Why did you deceive—

ANNABEL *(cutting him off)*. Father sent me away to recover at our house in the country. I tried to write to you, but Father intercepted my letters which made him all the more determined that I would never see you again.

POE. The only letter I received was the one from your father.

ANNABEL. Announcing my death?

POE. Yes, and the details of your funeral. He said because of the fever it had to be done without delay.

ANNABEL. But of course, there had been no funeral...

POE. But I knelt at your grave, I touched the tombstone there.

ANNABEL. Father was very thorough. He knew you would come so he had a grave prepared in our family plot, and a stone placed there for me...It is there still, next to Father, waiting for me...

POE. Why didn't you tell me the truth?...

ANNABEL. I didn't know the truth, not then. You see, I still longed for you but I thought you had left without a word. That's what my father had told me. I grew pale and melancholy, near death, in fact. Finally, one night I learned the truth from a kindly servant who took pity on me and told me the whole story.

POE. Why didn't you write to me?

ANNABEL. I tried, but the only way I knew to reach you was through your commanding officer at Ft. Moultrie, but all he could tell me was that you had gone back to Boston.

POE. But surely you could have written to me there.

ANNABEL. To whom? Edgar Perry?...You deceived me, too, Eddie...Why did you change your name?

POE. To keep my stepfather from finding me...

ANNABEL. It kept me from finding you, too. I never knew you were Edgar Allan Poe until *The Gold Bug* was published...An etching of you appeared in *The Mercury*, with a note that you had once been stationed at Ft. Moultrie.

POE. Why didn't you write to me then?

ANNABEL. I inquired but I learned you were married.

POE. I loved her very much...but she's gone now.

ANNABEL. I know.

POE. And did you find someone else?

ANNABEL. No, there was no one else for me. I never married. It was my quiet revenge against my father...denying him grandchildren.

POE. And your father?

ANNABEL. He died last year...

POE. And you gained your freedom...

ANNABEL. Freedom?...No, I am still buried deep in our family vault...my heart cold and hard as marble.

POE. Sounds like one of my stories.

ANNABEL. Yes, doesn't it?

POE. So, then, why have your brought me here?

ANNABEL. It is you who have brought me here...

POE. So what must I do now...

ANNABEL. That's up to you. *(She removes one of the dust covers from a table. Beneath it is a writing desk, paper, ink and pen ready. She hands him the pen. POE slowly sits at the desk, takes the pen and begins to write. As he does ANNABEL crosses U. As she raises the hood on her costume and passes behind one of the shrouded pieces of furniture, she switches places with NIMROD who is dressed in a hood exactly like hers. POE [and audience] does not realize the switch has been made.)*

POE. I could scarcely believe it. After all these years to be back in Charleston, that mystical kingdom by the sea, with Annabel, who across time and circumstance had reached out, like an angel bending low from the heavens above. Could this be another cruel hoax being played out on me... is she real or am I once more simply imagining?

*(Suddenly the Raven cries out. As it does, POE turns to look off and up at it. When he turns back, the figure of ANNABEL LEE turns around and we see that she has been transformed into NIMROD.)*

CAPTAIN NIMROD. Writing again, Edgar?

POE. Nimrod!

CAPTAIN NIMROD *(takes pages from POE)*. So, how's it going?

POE. Quite well, actually...

CAPTAIN NIMROD *(looks over POE's writings)*. Hmm-mm...*(Reads.)* Once upon a midnight dreary, while I pondered...

POE. It doesn't say that.

CAPTAIN NIMROD. But it does...*(He hands pages back to POE. POE takes them, looks at the first page and sees that it contains, not what he has written, but lines from* The Raven. *Quickly he looks over the other pages. They, too, only contain lines from* The Raven.*)*

POE. You've tricked me, again.

CAPTAIN NIMROD. Have I? Or have you tricked yourself, again? *(The Raven cries. POE moves D to address it. The D curtain falls and NIMROD disappears behind it.)*

POE. No, you're the trickster, aren't you? Why? Why? What is it you want? Why have you pursued me all this way?... Is this your revenge...for my giving you wing? Is that it, revenge?...Revenge that I caged you in verse and bound you in parchment...Is that it?...Is that it? All right, all right...*(He rips up the pages. The D curtain rises and Poe's cabin has disappeared and the bow of the ship is once again seen U. A violent storm is building.)* Then here, here...if you want your freedom... here...I'll give you your freedom then...I'll give it to you then...*(He races to the bow. and throws the papers overboard.)* There...

### SCENE 18: Descent into a Maelstrom

*On the Ship*

*(SEAMEN enter looking for POE.)*

JAKE. There he is!
REYNOLDS. Where...
MIKE. Up there on the bow.

REYNOLDS *(struggling along one of the lifelines to reach the bow).* Edgar, we've been looking everywhere for you, are you all right?

POE. Our descent into the mouth of hell has begun...You'll not take me with you! *(He climbs out onto the bow of the ship.)*

REYNOLDS. Edgar, we must get below till the storm blows over...

POE. This is no storm. This is the Gateway to Hell...The Maelstrom...

REYNOLDS *(shouting over the wind).* No, Edgar, it's an old-fashioned northeaster...Come down from there...

POE. Liar...I can see the swirling whirlpool below...

CAPTAIN NIMROD. The man is mad...

REYNOLDS. Come down, Edgar...

POE. No, I must escape...I must return to my destiny...An-nabel...Annabel. You said I only had to call for you and...

MRS. PROTHERO. Who's he calling for?

MRS. REILLY. I don't know.

POE. Annabel, I'm calling for you...*(The moon appears U in the fog.)* There...she's there...

MIKE. He's going to jump.

MRS. PROTHERO. Oh my God...

CABIN BOY 1. Don't jump, Mr. Poe!

RUSTY. Don't...

POE. The light...See it?...It's a sign. Annabel, my Annabel Lee...

REYNOLDS. It's just the moon, breaking through the storm clouds.

POE. Annabel...I won't doubt you again...Here, take my hand...

CAPTAIN NIMROD. Don't do it, man! *(POE prepares to jump.)*

REYNOLDS. Edgar, nooooooooooooo *(The ship begins to break up.)*

JAKE. Look out, we're losing the mainsail...*(The WOMEN scream. The mainsail falls.)*

REYNOLDS. What's happening?

*(CABIN BOY 2 emerges from below.)*

CABIN BOY 2. We're taking on water below...

MIGUEL. The ship is breaking up...

POE. ...We must make our escape. *(POE leaps into the void. The ship breaks up into pieces, rigging and the mast fall, lights fade and the wind grows to a deafening roar. The D sail falls and the barroom is set up D of it.)*

### SCENE 19: Calm Yourself, Man

*Poe's Deathbed in the Back Room of a Bar in Baltimore*

*(The noise from the scene above segues into the sounds of a busy barroom. This is represented in silhouettes of the bar PATRONS which appear on the D sail. As the lights rise, Poe's deathbed is seen. POE cries out with a blood-curdling scream. The silhouetted characters are silenced and look D toward the scream. The BARTENDER makes motions to the crowd that everything is all right and that he is going to check on things. He comes around the sail, as if to a back room, and as he does, lights D of the sail rise and we see two GENTLEMEN in the back room of the bar trying to restrain POE. Standing nearby is one of the BARMAIDS.)*

MR. QUERY. Calm yourself, man...

POE. He's after me, don't you see...

MR. QUERY. There is no one after you...

POE. Demon, he's a demon...

BARMAID. There are no demons here...

POE. He's in league with the devil for my soul...

BARTENDER. Get ahold of yourself, Mr. Poe...You were ill, wandering the streets and the police brought you here...

POE *(calming down)*. Wandering?

BARTENDER. Mr. Query here says he took you to the dock five days ago to board a ship for New York. Obviously, you did not make it there.

POE. I've been on a voyage...a nightmarish voyage...

MR. QUERY. Yes, but can you tell us where you have been?

POE. *Terra incognita*...

MR. QUERY. Where's that?

POE. Annabel...have you seen her?...

MR. QUERY. Who?

POE. Annabel Lee...

BARMAID *(as the MEN look to her)*. There is no one here by that name...

POE. She was there...*(POE faints.)*

MR. QUERY. He's been ranting like this for hours. Ah! Here are the doctors...

*(DOCTOR NICOLAI and DOCTOR FLEMING enter from the stormy night outside.)*

POE. They're demons...back...stay away from me...

BARTENDER. Mr. Poe, it's only Doctor Fleming and Doctor Nicolai...

POE. Doctors, why do I need doctors?

BARTENDER. We bound him to the bed. We didn't know what else to do.

MR. QUERY. You are ill, Edgar...

POE. Ill, I'm not ill...

DOCTOR NICOLAI. Why don't you let us decide that... *(POE is terrified but he looks to the BARMAID. She nods her head as if to say "Yes, it's all right.")*

POE. I have the most fearful dreams...Do you think, perhaps I could have a drop of brandy? Perhaps a drop of brandy would...

DOCTOR FLEMING. I fear, sir, brandy may be part of your problem. *(He prepares a draft of medicine.)*

BARTENDER. Let's wait outside...*(Exits, and ushers others out with him.)*

POE *(grabs FLEMING by the neck)*. You must help me, Doctor. I trust no one. They're all after me, demons, you see...

DOCTOR FLEMING. Take this...Take it...It will ease your dreams...*(POE drinks.)*

POE. What is it?

DOCTOR FLEMING. Poison, Edgar...*(He pulls back his hood and we see that he is actually REYNOLDS.)*

POE. Jeremiah!

REYNOLDS. I'm sorry, Eddie...

POE. Sorry? *(He gasps as the poison begins to take effect.)*

REYNOLDS. Don't despair. It is very quick-acting and there will be little pain...

POE. No...

REYNOLDS. There's not really enough to kill you, you see...

CAPTAIN NIMROD [NICOLAI]. Just enough to make you fall into a deep sleep so that your body will imitate death...

POE. Imitate death...Then what?...

CAPTAIN NIMROD. Then...

DOCTOR FLEMING [REYNOLDS]. You will be buried alive...

POE. No...

CAPTAIN REYNOLDS. I warned you what it would be like if you didn't give in, Eddie...

DOCTOR NICOLAI [NIMROD]. It will be over in a few hours...

POE (*gasping for breath*). A few hours?

REYNOLDS. Yes. In a few hours you will awaken in your earthly tomb and then asphyxiation will begin...

POE. Why do you do this to me?

REYNOLDS. I simply couldn't let you escape, Edgar. Then I would lose my own way out.

CAPTAIN NIMROD. We told you your nightmares would never cease until you gave in...next stop...The Premature Burial...

POE. Monster...

DOCTOR FLEMING [REYNOLDS]. Good night, Eddie.

POE. You of all people, Reynolds...how could you turn on— (*A sharp pain hits him.*) Meeeeeeeeeeeeeeeeeeee!

(*POE lunges for the DOCTORS, others enter and restrain him. All ad lib... "What's wrong?"... etc.*)

POE. Monster...They poisoned me...Don't you see, they... (*The poison does its work.*) They...poisoned me...(*He utters a bloodcurdling scream.*) Noooooooooooooooo-oooooo! (*POE collapses.*)

BARTENDER. Gone?

DOCTOR NICOLAI [NIMROD] (*checks POE's heart*). Gone.

DOCTOR FLEMING [REYNOLDS]. It was drink that poisoned him.

MR. QUERY. No doubt. No doubt.

*(Others shake their heads. Music. A sheet is pulled over POE's body. PALLBEARERS appear down the aisle of the theatre. They bring the wooden coffin they are carrying up onto the apron, then they cross up to Poe's bed and lift his body, still covered by the sheet, onto a stretcher which they also brought with them. They bring the stretcher D to the coffin and as they do, the D sail flies in. While they lift Poe's body into the coffin and nail the lid shut, the barroom is struck and the graveyard set up.)*

## SCENE 20: The Bells

*(Hand bells, rung by MOURNERS, begin tolling offstage. The D sail rises revealing the gravesite, which is actually the UC hatch of the ship. Standing U of it are a PRIEST, an ACOLYTE, and a GRAVEDIGGER with a wheelbarrow of earth and a shovel. The PALLBEARERS bring the coffin forward to the grave. MOURNERS, carrying hand bells, enter from L and R. The hand bells are rung randomly throughout the reciting of the bells. Care should be taken that the bells are rung at the ends of lines so the words are not lost.)*

PRIEST.

    Hear the tolling of the bells—
    Iron bells
    What a world of solemn thought their melody compels
    In the silence of the night
    How we shiver with affright
    At the melancholy menace of their tone
    For every sound that floats

From the rust within their throats
Is a groan.
And the people—ah, the people—

MALE MOURNER 1.
  Keeping time, time, time
  In a sort of runic rhyme,

FEMALE MOURNER 4.
  To the tintinnabulation that so musically wells
  From the

| FEMALE MOURNER 1. | Bells |
| MALE MOURNER 2. | Bells |
| FEMALE MOURNER 4. | Bells |
| MALE MOURNER 1. | Bells |
| FEMALE MOURNER 5. | Bells |
| MALE MOURNER 3. | Bells |
| MALE MOURNER 4. | Bells... |
| PRIEST. | ...from the jingling and tinkling of the bells |

FEMALE MOURNER 3.
  Hear the loud alarum bells—

FEMALE MOURNER 4.
  Brazen bells...

FEMALE MOURNER 3.
  What a tale of terror, now, their turbulency tells!

FEMALE MOURNER 4.
  In the startled ear of night
  How they scream out their affright!

FEMALE MOURNER 3.
>Too much horrified to speak,
>They can only shriek, shriek,

PRIEST.
>Out of tune

| | |
|---|---|
| MALE MOURNER 2. | [And the] bells |
| MALE MOURNER 1. | Bells |
| MALE MOURNER 2. | Bells |

MALE MOURNER 4.
>What a tale their terror tells...

FEMALE MOURNER 3.
>Of despair...

MALE MOURNER 2.
>How they clang, and clash and roar!

MALE MOURNER 4.
>What a horror they outpour...

| | |
|---|---|
| FEMALE MOURNER 6. | ...hear] the sobbing of the bells; |
| MALE MOURNER 1. | Keeping time, time, time |
| FEMALE MOURNER 4. | In a happy runic rhyme, |
| FEMALE MOURNER 3. | To the rolling of the bells— |
| MALE MOURNER 3. | Of the bells, bells, bells |
| MALE MOURNER 1. | To the tolling of the bells, |
| FEMALE MOURNER 3. | Of the bells |
| ALL. | bells, bells, (FM 4) bells, |
| | (MM 5) bells, (FM 5) bells, |
| | (MM 2) bells, (MM 4) bells |

PRIEST.              To the moaning and the groaning of the bells.

*(The coffin, which has remained in full view of the audience, is lowered into the grave and covered with dirt. The grave is a cross-section so that we still see the coffin, even after it is buried. PALLBEARERS exit. MOURNERS cross D, leaving the gravesite.)*

FEMALE MOURNER 5. Drink, they say.

FEMALE MOURNER 4. A shame.

FEMALE MOURNER 6. Yes.

FEMALE MOURNER 3. I hear they found him in the gutter..

MALE MOURNER 4. Wandering about, delirious he was, talking out of his head.

FEMALE MOURNER 3. We recognized him...

MALE MOURNER 1. We took him in and sent for his relatives.

FEMALE MOURNER 5. Where'd he been?

FEMALE MOURNER 4. No one knows.

MALE MOURNER 4. Five days ago I saw him board a ship bound for New York...

FEMALE MOURNER 3. But they said he never arrived.

FEMALE MOURNER 4. Where was he all that time?

FEMALE MOURNER 5. No one knows...

MALE MOURNER 1. It's a mystery...

FEMALE MOURNER 4. How appropriate

FEMALE MOURNER 5. Agnes...

FEMALE MOURNER 4. Well, it is.

FEMALE MOURNER 3. Poor wretch...

*(The GRAVEDIGGER completes his task by shoveling several shovelfulls of sand onto the grave. He is about to leave when he notices a mysterious LADY appear. Dressed in a black hood and cape, she approaches the grave. After*

*a moment there emerges, from beneath her cloak, a beautiful lace-gloved hand which places a single white rose and a bottle of cognac on the grave.)*

GRAVEDIGGER. Did you know him?

LADY. Once…

GRAVEDIGGER. You loved him once?

LADY. I love him still…

GRAVEDIGGER. Still?

LADY *(has reached down to take a handful of earth and as she speaks, she lets it fall through her hands and onto the grave).* We loved with a love that was more than love…

GRAVEDIGGER *(reaches out and catches the last few grains of sand falling from her hand).* I…and my Annabel Lee.

LADY [ANNABEL LEE]. Eddie?

GRAVEDIGGER [POE]. Annabel. *(He takes her hand and they meet at the head of the grave.)*

ANNABEL. But I thought you…

POE. Lost faith…yes…I doubted the power of my own imagination…the voice of my own soul…I won't doubt again…

  For Neither the angels in Heaven Above

    Nor the demons under the sea,

  Can ever dissever my soul from the soul

    Of the beautiful Annabel Lee…

ANNABEL. Can this really be happening? Can it really be true?

POE. We must make our own truth, remember…

ANNABEL. I remember, but how—?

POE. I wrote a new ending…

*(They kiss passionately. Lights crossfade leaving them in silhouette. At the same time, lights rise D on the coffin, drawing our attention to it. The sound of splintering wood is heard and a hand appears out of the top of the coffin.*

*From the glove on its hand, we know it is REYNOLDS. The hand becomes more and more desperate, its owner slowly suffocating, and then, as death comes, the hand is stilled.)*

LIGHTS FADE—CURTAIN

# THE FACTS ARE THESE

Edgar Allan Poe did disappear for five days prior to his death, his whereabouts and activities are completely unknown. It is believed he boarded a ship for New York but even that is not absolutely certain.

We do know that he was found delirious, wandering the streets of Baltimore. Recognized by an acquaintance, he was taken to a nearby tavern and a doctor friend of Poe's sent for. The doctor and Poe's relatives arranged for Poe's transfer to nearby Washington Hospital.

Throughout the night that followed, Poe remained delirious and delusional. Long into the night he called out, over and over again, for someone named "Reynolds," but no one there knew who that was. Finally, Poe was calmed down. Three days later, after fading in and out of consciousness, but without regaining coherence, he died.

His enemies and literary rivals were quick to blame Poe's drinking on his demise. There is no doubt, Poe had a problem with alcohol but many scholars believe that, in his last years, Poe was also battling with severe mental illness. After the death of his wife Virginia to tuberculosis, most agree, Poe was severely depressed and never the same again.

He did make an effort to stop drinking, even joining the Richmond Sons of Temperance, but soon he was drinking again. Many believe this led to Poe's madness although he himself said the drink didn't make him mad—the madness made him drink. Some scholars have suggested that Poe showed the symptoms of hypoglycemia, which would explain his low tolerance for alcohol and his delusional behavior at times. Whatever the diagnosis, Poe's mental condition was certainly severely impaired at the time of his death.

Who was the mysterious "Reynolds" to whom Poe called out? Many believe he was Jeremiah Reynolds, a minor Antarctic explorer of the 19th century. Reynolds, like many during this last age of exploration, believed that somewhere in the Antarctic region there was an entrance to the center of the earth, perhaps to a land of paradise. Poe used this theory and the journals Reynolds had written about his Antarctic expeditions in two of his stories. Both his short novel, *The Narrative of Arthur Gordon Pym* and *Manuscript Found in the Bottle* tell tales of ghostly, ghastly and ultimately ill-fated voyages to the Antarctic.

While the inspiration for Poe's fascination with the Antarctic can be traced to Jeremiah Reynolds, there is little solid information as to the identity of Annabel Lee. Poe's poem, *Annabel Lee*, was one of the last, perhaps *the* last poem Poe penned before his death. No one knows the identity of his beloved Annabel Lee, however. Perhaps she is someone biographers have failed to discover. Most likely she was a creature only of Poe's vivid imagination. Charleston author and publisher, Mrs. Elizabeth Verner Hamilton, in the Tradd Street Press's Sullivans Island Edition of *The Gold Bug*, speculates that perhaps Annabel Lee was a young Charleston belle who became Poe's first love. Poe was, after all, stationed at Sullivans Island when he was only seventeen, young, impressionable and adventurous. He had run away from home, joined the army under the alias Edgar A. Perry and found himself stationed at Ft. Moultrie on Sullivans Island. If, indeed, Annabel Lee was a Charleston girl, this would, of course, make Charleston the fabled "kingdom by the sea." This is all mere speculation, however. But wonderful speculation, so wonderful that I borrowed this premise for *Nevermore!*.

One final note. Since the 1950s, on the anniversary of Poe's death, a mysterious lady appears at the cemetery where Poe is buried. Each year, she appears at midnight and leaves a bottle of cognac and a single white rose on his grave. No one knows the identify of this ghostly visitor.

# Nevermore !
## Set plan

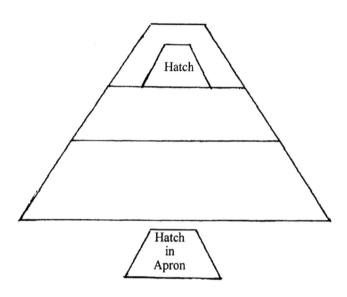

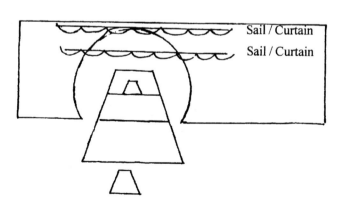

# NOTES ON STAGING

I am sure there are many scenic solutions which can be devised for the demands of *NEVERMORE!* and they need not be extremely complex. What is critical is that the changes from scene to scene happen with blinding swiftness or the magical, dream-within-a- dream sequences will fall flat. Here's how we solved the problems in the original production.

Because we wanted to give the sense that Poe was always on board a ship, the basic set was an abstract triangular wooden deck of a sailing vessel. It was wide near the apron of the stage and slanted upward to a narrow point upstage. There were two hatches, one far DC which was a trapdoor which descended into the orchestra pit and the other, UC which led to an area beneath the deck. The UC hatch, about 2 x 6 feet, could be closed for certain scenes. Late in the play, when open, it also served as Poe's grave.

The ship seemed to be sailing into a giant circle upstage which was sometimes filled with fog, at other times, swirling lights, or a projection of moon and stars, etc. For the Antarctic scenes a giant iceberg appeared there.

Hanging above the deck were two sets of curtains which were made to look, when raised, like the folded sails of the ship. One set of these sail curtains were downstage and the other set above 12 feet upstage. By raising and lowering them, scenes could be played in front of them while other scenes were being set up behind them. The sails were made of thin muslin and in many scenes the shadows of actors were projected onto them from upstage.

Most sets, therefore, consisted of simple furniture elements in front of the lowered sail curtains onto which projections or silhouettes were projected. The sails and projections added a mysterious and ephemeral element to the set.

## THE MAGIC TRICKS

### The Oblong Box

This is a standard false bottom magician's box. For a complete description see *Mark Wilson's Complete Book of Magic*.

### Poe's Escape from Death

This is very simple actually. Poe's deathbed was specially made so that his head appeared on the pillow but a trapdoor allowed for his body to be underneath the bed. The feet and body that the audience saw under the covers were actually those of another actor, whose identity was hidden by the covers. When Poe died, the sheet was pulled up over him and he slipped his head underneath the bed. The pillow covered the hole. It was the body of the second actor who was actually lifted off the bed, onto the stretcher and into the coffin. While this was happening a curtain fell hiding the bed. Poe then made his escape and took his place upstage as the Gravedigger. To speed up this change he was already wearing the Gravedigger's costume. Since the curtain rose only moments later, allowing just enough time for the bed to be taken off and Poe to get in place, the audience had no idea a switch had been made. We got great audience response from this trick.

## ABOUT THE POEMS

Poe was known to rewrite his poems, often changing their titles as well. The pieces used here in *NEVERMORE!* were taken from a volume in which the poems were reprinted from standard older editions, usually presenting the final versions, which are thought to be distinct improvements.

# DIRECTOR'S NOTES

# DIRECTOR'S NOTES

# DIRECTOR'S NOTES